Riding the Waves

A Century of the US stock Markets'
Generational Cycles

Brian S. Hoffman

Copyright 2024 by Brian S. Hoffman

All Rights Reserved.

No part of this publication may be reproduced, distributed, or transmitted in any form of by any means, including photocopying, recording, or other electronic methods, without the prior written permission of the publisher, except in the case of brief quotations embodied in critical reviews and certain other non-commercial uses permitted by copyright law.

PREFACE

The stock market has long been a source of fascination and frustration for investors worldwide. Throughout my two decades in the financial industry, I've witnessed firsthand the powerful impact of large market cycles—periods of significant growth followed by inevitable downturns. My journey into understanding these cycles began during the tumultuous years of the 2008 financial crisis when many lost their investments and confidence in the markets.

This book was born out of a desire to demystify the seemingly unpredictable stock market for my clients and, hopefully, any reader who comes across this book. It is my attempt to simplify all of the insane numbers investors encounter every day. I intend to add a perspective that goes beyond daily market fluctuations to explore the broader, recurring patterns that have shaped market behavior for centuries. To achieve this, I delved into historical data and events and analyzed economic indicators that signal shifts in market cycles. This cross-section of data, history, and psychology has led me to see that these large cycles last approximately 17 years. What we are talking about are not the 1,3,5 or even 10-year periods that most financial advisors reference. We are talking about Generational Cycles going back 100 years or more.

I owe a debt of gratitude first to my wife, Jennifer, as she has had to listen to my "interesting" stats and data for years. She is the light of my life and my partner in everything. To my girls, Emily and Sarah, who have provided me with the happiness it takes to get my thoughts straight. To my mentors and colleagues who shared their invaluable insights and supported me throughout this research. Lastly, to my clients, who have allowed me to drone on and on about US history, the markets, and the economy for years. Each of those conversations helped me put more context behind the next conversation. Their contributions have been instrumental in shaping the perspectives and strategies presented in this book.

My aim is to equip both novice and experienced investors with the tools and knowledge to identify and leverage these Generational Cycles, ultimately leading to more informed and strategic investment decisions. By understanding the rhythms of the market, you can better navigate its peaks and troughs, turning uncertainty into opportunity.

As you embark on this journey, I encourage you to approach each chapter with an open mind and a willingness to delve deeper into the forces that drive the stock market. Together, we will explore the intricate dance of economic factors, investor psychology, and historical trends that define the large cycles of the stock market.

Thank you for choosing this book as your guide. I hope it serves as a valuable resource on your path to financial mastery.

Table of Contents

PREFACE i
Chapter 1: Introduction 1
    1.1 Setting the Stage for Understanding the Stock Market's Historical Cycles 4
    1.2 Importance of Studying Boom and Bust Periods 6
    1.3 The Structure of Market Cycles 10
    1.4 Lessons for the Future 12
Chapter 2: The Roaring Twenties (1911-1928) 14
        Bull Market – Expansion 14
        Dow Jones Industrial 14
        January 1, 1911 - 81.68 14
        December 31, 1928 – 300 14
        1913-1914 Recession 16
        1920-1921 Recession 17
        1923-1924 Recession 18
        1926-1927 Recession 18
    2.1 The Economic and Market Conditions During the First Expansion 20
    2.1.1 Post-War Optimism 20
    2.1.2 Industrialization and Technological Advances 21
    2.1.3 Speculation and the Birth of the Bull Market 23

2.2 The Effects of World War I on the Market 25
2.2.1 Financing the War Effort 25
2.2.2 The Transition to a Global Superpower 27
2.3 The Great Depression of 1929 and Its Causes 28
2.3.1 The Stock Market Crash of 1929 28
2.3.2 Contributing Factors 29
2.3.3 The Domino Effect 30

Chapter 3: The Great Depression and World War II (1929-1946) 32

    Bear Market – Contraction 32

    Dow Jones Industrial 32

    January 1, 1929 – 300 32

    December 31, 1946 – 177 32

    Annualized DJIA Return (Dividends Reinvested) - 1.703% 33

    The Great Depression (1929-1933) 34

    Recession of 1937-1938 35

    Recession of 1945 35

    3.1 The Crash of 1929 and the Subsequent Market Collapse 37

    3.2 The New Deal and Government Interventions 40

    3.3 The Impact of World War II on the Economy and the Market 44

Chapter 4: Post-War Prosperity (1947-1964) 49

Bull Market – Expansion 49
Dow Jones Industrial 49
January 1, 1947 - 177 49
December 31, 1964 – 874.13 49
Recession of 1949 52
Recession of 1953 52
Recession of 1957-1958 53
Recession of 1960-1961 53
4.1 The Marshall Plan and the Recovery of Europe 54
4.2 The Baby Boomer Generation and Consumer Spending 58
4.3 Technological Innovations and the Rise of American Corporations 61
4.4 The Seeds of Future Challenges 65

Chapter 5: The Vietnam War, Stagflation and Social Upheaval (1965-1981) 69

Dow Jones Industrial 69
Flat or Neutral return 69
January 1, 1965 – 874.13 69
December 31, 1981 – 875 69
Recession of 1969-1970 72
1973-1975 Recession 72
1980 Recession... 73

    1981 Recession 73

    5.1 The Impact of the Vietnam War on the Economy 74

    5.2 Social and Political Upheaval: The Assassinations, Rights and Resignation 78

    5.2.1 The Voting Rights Act of 1965 78

    5.2.4 The Resignation of President Nixon 83

    5.3 The Oil Crisis and Stagflation 83

    5.4 The Rise of Interest Rates and Federal Reserve Policies 88

    5.5 The Transition to Reaganomics 90

Chapter 6: Reaganomics and the Bull Market 92

(1982-1999) 92

    Bull Market – Expansion 92

    Dow Jones Industrial 92

    January 1, 1982 - 875 92

    December 31, 1999 – 11497.12 92

    Early 1990s Recession 94

    6.1 The Reagan Presidency and Supply-Side Economics 95

    6.2 The Bull Market of the 1980s and 1990s 99

    6.3 The Technology Boom of the 1990s 102

    6.4 The Effects of Globalization and Trade 104

    6.5 The Seeds of the Dot-Com Bust 107

Chapter 7: The Dot-Com Bust, 9/11 and the Great Recession (2000-2017) 109

    Bear Market – Contraction 109

    Dow Jones Industrial 109

    January 1, 2000 - 11497.12.. 109

    December 31, 2017 – 24719.22 109

    Early 2000s Recession (Dot-Com Bubble) 112

    Great Recession (2007-2009) 112

    7.1 The Bursting of the Dot-Com Bubble 114

    7.2 The Effects of the 9/11 Terrorist Attacks on the Market 118

    7.3 The Housing Bubble and Financial Crisis of 2008 123

    7.4 The Recovery and Economic Expansion (2009-2017) 130

Chapter 8: The New Millennium (2018-Today) 133

    Bull Market – Expansion 133

    Dow Jones Industrial 133

    January 1, 2018 – 24719.22 133

    COVID-19 Recession 135

    8.1 Economic Trends Leading Up to 2020 136

    8.2 The Impact of the COVID-19 Pandemic on the Market 139

    8.3 Economic Recovery and the Challenges of 2021-2022 144

8.4 The Future of the Stock Market and Global Economy 148

Conclusion: Learning from the Generational 152

Cycles 152

Introduction to the Cycles: Lessons from History 152

The Significance of the Cycles: Navigating Expansion and Contraction 153

Technological Innovation: AI and the Future of Productivity 155

The U.S. Economy's Resilience: Overcoming Adversity 157

The Generational Cycles: A Guide for Investors 158

Conclusion: Hopeful for the Future 160

Chapter 1
Introduction

The stock market, an ever-evolving and complex entity, has profoundly shaped the United States's economic history. Its powerful influence over wealth generation and financial stability has made it both a beacon of opportunity and a source of deep anxiety. Investors, policymakers, and economists have spent over a century trying to decode its patterns, searching for the underlying forces that drive its inevitable fluctuations. Central to these efforts is the recognition that the market moves in cycles—periods of boom followed by bust, expansion followed by contraction, prosperity followed by crisis.

These cycles, which tend to span approximately 17 years, I refer to as "generational cycles," as they often align with the social and economic shifts experienced by successive generations. It's important to note that this is an approximation when I speak of 17 years. In some cases, I refer to 18-year periods. I aim not to pinpoint the exact dates when the markets bottom out or shift direction but to identify and understand the broader trends. Many respected authorities have weighed in on the duration of these cycles—Kerry Balenthiran, for example, in *The 17.6 Year Stock Market Cycle,* delves into the data, describing cycles within cycles and identifying 2.2- and 4.4-year bull market trends that culminate in euphoria. Warren Buffett, too, has discussed 17-year cycles more generally. Even research suggests that commodities follow an 18-year bull and bear cycle.

While this book acknowledges these finer points of market analysis, my goal is to take a step back. Rather than getting bogged down in granular data, I will focus on the larger generational cycles, typically spanning 17-18 years, using the Dow Jones Industrial Average as our primary data point. The Dow has been around the longest, and when most people think of "the market," they often think of the Dow.

However, more than providing technical analysis, my primary aim in writing this book is to offer perspective. Data, numbers, and worries surround us, and it's easy to get lost in the noise. By examining the broader cycles of the market, I hope to offer insight into what we can learn from the past. We'll explore the history of the U.S. and its markets, focusing on the recurring challenges that have tested us over the past century or more—some of which we remember vividly, others we may have forgotten or never even heard of. Yet through it all, the market, like the nation, has shown resilience. We've continued to move forward and thrive.

As I often tell my clients, many of the fears and uncertainties we face today are not new—they have occurred before. But as we age, our relationship with these events changes. When we're in our 50s, 60s, or 70s, we've gained more and therefore have more to lose than when we were 20. The fear of loss becomes more real, and today's challenges seem more acute than those of the 1960s or 1970s. This is where perspective becomes critical. By zooming out and looking at the bigger picture, we see the patterns and cycles that have defined the market over the past 100+ years.

In this book, *Riding the Waves: A Century of the US Stock Market's Generational Cycles (1910–2023)*, we explore how these 18-year cycles have shaped the landscape of the U.S. stock market and the broader economy. By examining key historical events—ranging from the Roaring Twenties to the

Dot-Com Bubble, from the Great Depression to the 2008 financial crisis—we will uncover the lessons these cycles offer and explore how they continue to influence modern market dynamics. The purpose of this book is not just to recount history but to provide a framework for understanding how these generational cycles can inform future investment decisions and economic policy.

1.1 Setting the Stage for Understanding the Stock Market's Historical Cycles

Before delving into the intricacies of the stock market's historical cycles, it is essential to establish a foundation of knowledge regarding how the market functions. At its core, the stock market is a place where publicly traded companies' shares are bought and sold. These transactions occur on exchanges like the New York Stock Exchange (NYSE) or the NASDAQ, where prices are determined by supply and demand. Investors, ranging from large institutional players such as pension funds to individual retail investors, interact within this marketplace to capitalize on short-term price movements or build wealth over the long term.

The value of a stock is influenced by a range of factors, including a company's earnings, growth prospects, and the overall economic environment. However, as history has shown, stock prices are not always tied directly to a company's intrinsic value. Market sentiment, investor psychology, and external events (such as geopolitical tensions or technological breakthroughs) often play a significant role in driving prices up or down. This disconnect between fundamental value and price is a key feature of the boom-and-bust cycles that characterize the stock market.

Historically, the U.S. stock market has experienced cycles of expansion (bull markets) and contraction (bear markets). Various factors, including technological advancements, economic policy changes, investor sentiment, and major world events, drive these cycles. Importantly, these cycles are not random; they often follow recognizable patterns that can be traced over time. By examining these patterns, we can gain insights into the forces that shape market behavior and better understand how to navigate future cycles.

One of the key ideas explored in this book is the concept of the generational cycle, which spans approximately 18 years. This cycle captures the ebbs and flows of the stock market, reflecting broader societal and economic shifts that occur across generations. Each generation—whether shaped by war, economic prosperity, or technological innovation—tends to experience a unique set of circumstances that influence market dynamics. Understanding these generational cycles can provide valuable insights into market behavior, helping investors make informed decisions and policymakers develop effective economic strategies.

1.2 Importance of Studying Boom and Bust Periods

Why should we study boom and bust periods? This question lies at the heart of our exploration. At first glance, market cycles may seem like mere historical curiosities—interesting but irrelevant to the modern investor or policymaker. However, this perspective overlooks the valuable lessons that these cycles offer. Studying boom and bust periods is not just about understanding the past; it is about recognizing the patterns that repeat over time and learning how to navigate the future more confidently.

One of the most important lessons gleaned from studying market cycles is how boom periods often lead to overconfidence and risk-taking. During expansions, investors become increasingly optimistic about the future, often pushing stock prices to unsustainable levels. This behavior was evident during the Roaring Twenties, the Dot-Com Bubble, and the housing market boom leading to the 2008 financial crisis. In each case, the market surged as investors poured money into speculative assets, convinced that the good times would never end. Yet, as history has shown time and time again, these periods of exuberance inevitably give way to busts, as speculative bubbles burst and asset prices come crashing down.

Conversely, bust periods expose vulnerabilities and systemic flaws within the economy. These downturns often reveal underlying weaknesses in corporate governance, financial regulation, or investment strategies that had been overlooked or ignored during the boom. For example, the stock market crash of 1929 laid bare the dangers of unregulated margin trading and speculative investment, leading to the creation of new regulatory frameworks like the Securities and Exchange Commission (SEC). Similarly, the 2008 financial crisis highlighted the risks associated with complex financial products like mortgage-backed securities and the dangers of an underregulated banking system.

Government intervention and regulation often play a critical role during bust periods. The New Deal reforms of the 1930s, which introduced social safety nets and strengthened financial regulation, are a prime example of how government action can stabilize a collapsing economy. In more recent times, the Dodd-Frank Act, passed in the aftermath of the 2008 crisis, aimed to curb the excesses of Wall Street by increasing oversight of financial institutions. However, the effectiveness of government interventions is often debated. Some argue that regulation stifles innovation and imposes unnecessary burdens on businesses, while others contend that a strong regulatory framework is essential for maintaining market stability.

In addition to offering lessons for policymakers, the study of boom and bust cycles provides valuable insights for investors. One of the most important strategies for navigating market volatility is diversification—spreading investments across various asset classes and sectors to mitigate risk. During boom periods, it can be tempting to chase high returns by concentrating investments in rapidly appreciating sectors, such as technology stocks, during the Dot-Com Bubble. However, as history has shown, this approach can lead to significant losses when the bubble bursts. By maintaining a diversified portfolio, investors can reduce their exposure to market downturns and protect themselves against the worst effects of a bust.

Market cycles also have profound social and political implications. During boom periods, wealth inequality often increases as those with access to capital benefit disproportionately from rising stock prices. Conversely, bust periods can exacerbate social issues like unemployment and poverty, leading to political instability and shifts in public policy. The Great Depression of the 1930s, for example, led to a surge in support for populist political movements and a greater emphasis on government intervention in the economy. Similarly, the aftermath of the 2008 financial crisis saw increased public scrutiny of Wall Street and a renewed debate over the role of government in regulating the financial system.

Finally, studying historical market cycles offers important lessons for the future. By recognizing the recurring patterns that have shaped the stock market over the past century, we can better anticipate and prepare for future market fluctuations. While it is impossible to predict exactly when the next boom or bust will occur, understanding the forces that drive these cycles can help investors and policymakers make more informed decisions.

1.3 The Structure of Market Cycles

Stock market cycles typically consist of four distinct phases: expansion, peak, contraction, and trough. Each phase is marked by unique characteristics that influence investor behavior and economic activity. By understanding these phases, we can better understand where the market is headed and how to position ourselves accordingly.

1. **Expansion**: During the expansion phase, the economy is growing, corporate profits are rising, and investor confidence is high. Stock prices tend to increase during this period as investors anticipate future growth. The expansion phase can last several years, as was during the 1990s tech boom or the early 2000s housing market rally. Central banks often keep interest rates low during this time to encourage borrowing and investment.

2. **Peak**: The peak phase occurs when the market reaches its highest point of growth. Stock prices are often inflated, and investor sentiment is euphoric. At this point, many investors believe that the market will continue to rise indefinitely, leading to increased speculation and risk-taking. This is when a "herding mentality" can take over. Herding is when individuals who are traditionally risk adverse tend to push their worries aside and move with the crowd. We witnessed this in 1928 and 1929 when even those without the means became "investors". However, warning signs—such as rising interest rates, slowing economic growth, or declining corporate earnings—may begin to appear. These signs often go ignored during the peak phase, as investors remain focused on the market's upward momentum.

3. **Contraction**: The contraction phase, or bear market, follows the peak. Stock prices begin to fall as economic growth slows, corporate profits decline, and investor sentiment turns pessimistic. Many investors rush to sell their holdings to minimize losses during this phase, exacerbating the market's downward spiral. Various

factors, including rising interest rates, geopolitical instability, or financial crises, can trigger contractions. The contraction phase can last for several months or even years, as was the case during the Great Depression and the aftermath of the 2008 financial crisis.

4. **Trough**: The trough phase marks the bottom of the market cycle. At this point, stock prices have fallen to their lowest levels, and investor sentiment is typically at its most negative. However, the trough also presents opportunities for savvy investors who can recognize undervalued assets and invest at a discount. As the economy recovers, the market enters a new expansion phase, completing the cycle.

1.4 Lessons for the Future

As we explore the U.S. stock market's generational cycles, it is important to remember that history does not repeat itself exactly—but it does often rhyme. The boom and bust cycles of the past offer valuable lessons for the future, highlighting the risks of speculative excess, the importance of sound regulation, and the benefits of a diversified investment strategy. By studying these cycles, we can better prepare for the challenges that lie ahead, whether in the form of technological disruption, geopolitical conflict, or economic instability.

In the following chapters, we will delve deeper into the specific historical events that have shaped the U.S. stock market over the past century. From the exuberance of the Roaring Twenties to the devastation of the Great Depression, from the optimism of the post-war boom to the uncertainty of the 21st century, we will trace the patterns of expansion and contraction that have defined each generation's experience with the stock market. By understanding these patterns, we can ride the waves of the market with greater confidence and insight, navigating both the highs and the lows with a clear sense of direction.

Chapter 2
The Roaring Twenties (1911-1928)

Bull Market – Expansion

Dow Jones Industrial

January 1, 1911 - 81.68

December 31, 1928 – 300

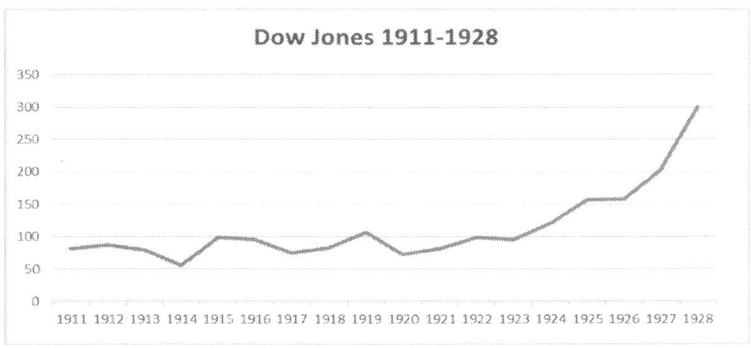

Total Dow Jones Industrial Average Return – 237.841%

Annualized Dow Jones Industrial Average Return – 7.031%

Total DJIA Return (Dividends Reinvested) – 836.007%

Annualized DJIA Return (Dividends Reinvested) – 13.295%[1]

- **New Highs**: 16 significant highs.
    - The Dow Jones saw several new highs, particularly in the 1920s during the economic boom after World War I.
    - The most notable high occurred in **1929**, just before the stock market crash, with the Dow reaching **381.17**.
- **New Lows**: 0 significant lows.
    - No significant lows were recorded during this period, though the market experienced volatility as it grew steadily.

Major Events:

- **1912 Presidential Election**: November 5, 1912 – Woodrow Wilson was elected President.
- **World War I**: July 28, 1914 – November 11, 1918 (U.S. entered on April 6, 1917).
- **Spanish Flu**: 1918

---

[1] Data - www.dqydj.com/dow-jones-return-calculator/

- **Red Summer**: 1919 – Period of severe racial riots and violence.
- **Treaty of Versailles**: Signed on June 28, 1919 – Officially ended World War I.
- **First Red Scare**: 1919-1920 – Fear of communism led to raids and arrests.
- **Prohibition**: January 16, 1919 - 18th Amendment passed.
- **1920 Presidential Election**: November 2, 1920 – Warren G. Harding was elected President.
- **19th Amendment**: Ratified on August 18, 1920 – Women gained the right to vote.
- **Harding's Death**: August 2, 1923 – President Warren G. Harding died; Calvin Coolidge became President.
- **1928 Presidential Election**: November 6, 1928 – Herbert Hoover was elected President.

Recessions and the Markets:

1913-1914 Recession

- **Duration**: January 1913 – December 1914 (23 months).

- **Stock Market Impact**:
    - The Dow declined by approximately 30% during the outbreak of World War I.
    - The NYSE was closed for four months starting in July 1914 to prevent panic selling due to the war.

Post-World War I Recession (1918-1919)

- **Duration**: August 1918 – March 1919 (7 months).
- **Stock Market Impact**:
    - The stock market was volatile but generally positive following the war's end, as optimism about the U.S. economy grew.
    - The DJIA gained around 10% in 1919 as the economy transitioned back to peacetime production.

1920-1921 Recession

- **Duration**: January 1920 – July 1921 (18 months)

- **Stock Market Impact**:
    o The DJIA dropped approximately 47% from late 1919 to mid-1921 due to deflation and high unemployment.
    o After the recession ended, the market began a strong recovery, leading to the Roaring Twenties.

1923-1924 Recession

- **Duration**: May 1923 – July 1924 (14 months)
- **Stock Market Impact**:
    o During the recession, the Dow saw relatively small declines, around 7%.
    o The market quickly recovered in late 1924 as economic growth resumed.

1926-1927 Recession

- **Duration**: October 1926 – November 1927 (13 months)

- **Stock Market Impact**:
    - The stock market remained resilient during the recession, with the Dow continuing to climb, gaining 40% in 1927.
    - Investors remained optimistic about the economy despite economic contraction.

The Roaring Twenties, often remembered as a period of unprecedented economic growth and cultural change, was when the United States experienced a dramatic expansion in its economy and stock market. It was an era defined by optimism, technological innovation, and speculation, but also one that culminated in the devastating collapse of 1929.

This chapter explores the economic and market conditions that characterized the first major expansion of the 20th century, the effects of World War I on the U.S. economy, and the factors that led to the catastrophic stock market crash at the end of the decade.

2.1 The Economic and Market Conditions During the First Expansion

Between 1910 and 1928, American history witnessed one of the most exhilarating phases of economic growth. Following the conclusion of World War I, the United States found itself in a unique position of economic strength. Unlike Europe, which was struggling to recover from the devastation of the war, the U.S. had emerged relatively unscathed and was poised to dominate the global economy. This newfound dominance laid the foundation for an era of rapid industrialization, technological advancement, and speculative investment.

2.1.1 Post-War Optimism

The end of World War I in 1918 marked the beginning of a new era for the United States. As soldiers returned home from the battlefields of Europe, they were greeted with an economy that was ready to expand. The war had driven significant advancements in manufacturing, as industries had been retooled to meet the demands of the military. With peace restored, these same industries shifted their focus to producing goods for civilian consumption.

The reintegration of millions of soldiers into the workforce was remarkably smooth, as the post-war economy experienced a surge in demand for goods and services. With Europe struggling to rebuild, American industries faced little competition, and the country quickly became the world's leading industrial power. This period of economic expansion was fueled by a sense of optimism and confidence in the future, as Americans believed that the prosperity of the post-war years would continue indefinitely. This sense of optimism was reflected in consumer spending. With wages rising and credit becoming more accessible, Americans began purchasing new consumer goods such as automobiles, radios, and household appliances. These products, which had once been luxuries reserved for the wealthy, were now within reach of the average American family. The growth in consumer spending drove the economy and contributed to the expansion of the stock market, as companies that produced these goods saw their stock prices soar.

2.1.2 Industrialization and Technological Advances

At the heart of the Roaring Twenties was a period of rapid industrialization and technological innovation. The decade saw the rise of new industries, the expansion of mass production techniques, and the widespread adoption of new technologies that transformed everyday life.

One of the most significant developments of the 1920s was the rise of the automobile industry, led by pioneers like Henry Ford. Ford's introduction of the assembly line revolutionized manufacturing, making it possible to produce cars more quickly and affordably than ever before. By the mid-1920s, the automobile had become a symbol of American prosperity and independence, with millions of families purchasing cars for the first time. The growth of the automobile industry had far-reaching effects on the economy, creating jobs in related sectors such as steel, rubber, oil, and construction. It also spurred the development of new infrastructure, including roads and highways, to accommodate the growing number of cars on the road.

In addition to the automobile, other technological innovations helped drive economic growth during the 1920s. The widespread adoption of electricity revolutionized industries and households, powering new appliances such as refrigerators, washing machines, and vacuum cleaners. The radio, which became a staple of American life during this decade, provided entertainment and created new opportunities for advertising and communication.

The industrial and technological advances of the 1920s were accompanied by a shift in how businesses were organized and managed. Large corporations, many of which had grown rapidly during the war, became more dominant in the economy. Companies like General Motors, General Electric, and U.S. Steel became household names, and their stocks were among the most widely held on Wall Street. These corporations were able to take advantage of economies of scale, producing goods more efficiently and at lower costs, which in turn boosted their profits and stock prices.

2.1.3 Speculation and the Birth of the Bull Market

As the U.S. economy expanded and corporate profits soared, the stock market entered one of the most dramatic bull markets in history. By the mid-1920s, investors were flocking to Wall Street, eager to capitalize on the rapid rise in stock prices. The idea of making quick profits through stock market speculation became deeply ingrained in the public consciousness, and many Americans—ranging from wealthy financiers to middle-class workers—began investing in stocks.

One of the key factors driving the bull market was the widespread use of margin trading, a practice in which investors borrowed money to buy stocks. Margin trading allowed investors to amplify their gains by using leverage, meaning they could control a large number of shares with a relatively small amount of cash. While this strategy worked well during the market's ascent, it also increased the risk of catastrophic losses if stock prices were to fall. As more and more investors borrowed money to buy stocks, the market became increasingly overleveraged, setting the stage for a potential collapse.

Speculation in the stock market reached a fever pitch by the late 1920s. Many investors began buying stocks not based on the fundamental value of the companies they were investing in but on the belief that stock prices would continue to rise. This speculative bubble was fueled by a widespread optimism and the belief that the market could only go up. The media, financial analysts, and even prominent public figures reinforced this belief, with some declaring that a "new era" of perpetual prosperity had arrived.

However, as history has shown repeatedly, speculative bubbles are unsustainable. The rapid rise in stock prices during the Roaring Twenties was disconnected from the underlying economic fundamentals, and when the bubble eventually burst, the consequences were devastating.

2.2 The Effects of World War I on the Market

While the Roaring Twenties was a period of extraordinary economic growth for the United States, the impact of World War I on the American economy and stock market was more complex. The war had left Europe in ruins, and the U.S. emerged from the conflict as the world's dominant economic power. This shift in the global economic landscape had far-reaching effects on the U.S. economy and the financial markets.

2.2.1 Financing the War Effort

During World War I, the U.S. government financed its involvement in the conflict by issuing war bonds, known as

Liberty Bonds. These bonds were marketed as a patriotic duty, and millions of Americans purchased them to support the war effort. The sale of Liberty Bonds diverted capital away from the stock market and into government securities, as investors sought to contribute to the war effort while earning a safe return on their investment.

The issuance of war bonds profoundly affected investment patterns in the years following the war. As the war came to an end and the government began redeeming these bonds, a significant amount of capital flowed back into the financial markets. This influx of capital and the post-war economic boom contributed to the rapid rise in stock prices during the 1920s.

However, the war had also created significant imbalances in the global economy. European nations, burdened with war debts and struggling to rebuild, could not contribute meaningfully to global economic growth. This placed additional pressure on the U.S. economy, as American industries increasingly depended on domestic demand to sustain their growth.

2.2.2 The Transition to a Global Superpower

World War I marked a turning point in the global economic order, with the United States emerging as the world's dominant economic and financial power. Before the war, London had been the center of global finance, with the British pound serving as the world's primary reserve currency. However, the war severely weakened the British economy, and New York quickly replaced London as the world's financial capital. The U.S. dollar became the global reserve currency, and American banks and investors became more prominent in international finance.

The establishment of the Federal Reserve System in 1913 also played a crucial role in shaping the post-war economic landscape. The Federal Reserve was tasked with regulating the money supply and acting as a lender of last resort to stabilize the banking system. During the 1920s, the Federal Reserve kept interest rates relatively low, which helped fuel the economic expansion but also contributed to the speculative bubble in the stock market. As the U.S. became more integrated into the global economy, it became more vulnerable to external shocks. The economic turmoil in Europe and the imbalances created by the war made the U.S. economy increasingly fragile. While the Roaring Twenties appeared to be a period of unending prosperity, the underlying vulnerabilities in domestic and global economies would soon become apparent.

2.3 The Great Depression of 1929 and Its Causes

The stock market crash of 1929, which marked the end of the Roaring Twenties and the beginning of the Great Depression, is one of the most significant events in American financial history. The crash resulted from a combination of factors, including excessive speculation, overvaluation of stocks, and structural weaknesses in the banking system. The aftermath of the crash triggered a broader economic collapse that had far-reaching consequences for the U.S. and the world.

2.3.1 The Stock Market Crash of 1929

The stock market crash of 1929 did not occur all at once but rather unfolded over several weeks. The first signs of trouble appeared on October 24, 1929; a day known as Black Thursday. On this day, stock prices began to decline sharply, triggering panic among investors. In the following days, attempts to stabilize the market were unsuccessful, and the panic continued to spread.

The final collapse came on October 29, 1929—Black Tuesday—when the stock market suffered its largest single-day decline in history. Investors, many of whom had purchased stocks on margin, were forced to sell their holdings at a loss to meet margin calls, further driving down prices. By the end of the day, billions of dollars in wealth had been wiped out, and the stock market was in freefall.

2.3.2 Contributing Factors

Several factors contributed to the stock market crash of 1929. One of the most important was the speculative bubble that developed in the late 1920s. As stock prices rose, more and more investors jumped into the market, driving prices higher and creating a feedback loop of rising valuations. Many of these investors were using borrowed money to buy stocks, magnifying their gains and losses.

The overvaluation of stocks was another key factor. By 1929, stock prices had become detached from the underlying fundamentals of the companies they represented. Many companies were trading at prices far above their actual earnings potential, creating an unsustainable bubble. When investors began to realize that these stocks were overvalued, the selling frenzy began.

External factors, such as international trade tensions and the passage of the Smoot-Hawley Tariff Act in 1930, also played a role in exacerbating the crisis. The Smoot-Hawley Tariff Act, which raised tariffs on imported goods, led to a sharp decline in international trade, further weakening the global economy.

2.3.3 The Domino Effect

The stock market crash of 1929 triggered a broader economic collapse known as the Great Depression. As stock prices plummeted, banks that had lent money to investors began to fail, leading to a wave of bank closures across the country. With the banking system in disarray, businesses could not access the credit they needed to operate, leading to widespread bankruptcies and layoffs.

Unemployment soared, reaching nearly 25% by the early 1930s, and deflation took hold as prices fell in response to collapsing demand. The combination of high unemployment, falling prices, and a broken financial system created a vicious cycle that deepened the economic crisis.

The Roaring Twenties, which had been a period of exuberance and prosperity, ended in one of the darkest chapters of American history. The stock market crash of 1929 and the subsequent Great Depression served as a stark reminder of the dangers of speculative excess and the importance of sound economic and financial regulation.

Chapter 3
The Great Depression and World War II (1929-1946)

Bear Market – Contraction

Dow Jones Industrial

January 1, 1929 – 300

December 31, 1946 – 177

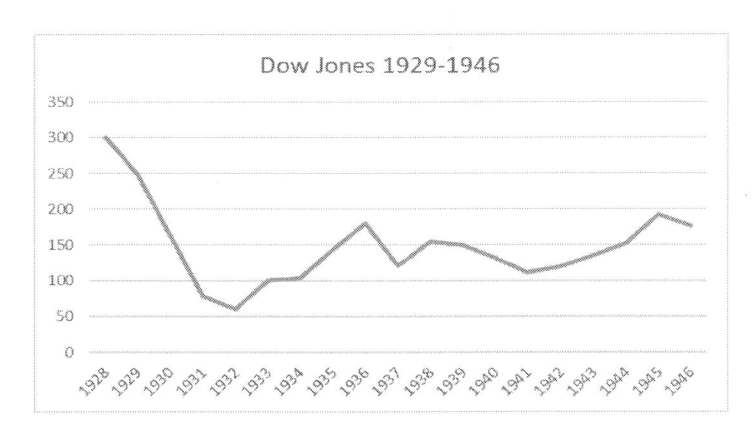

Dow Jones 1929-1946 chart

Total Dow Jones Industrial Average Return - -43.015%

Annualized Dow Jones Industrial Average Return - -3.09%

Total DJIA Return (Dividends Reinvested) – 35.325%

Annualized DJIA Return (Dividends Reinvested) - 1.703%[2]

- **New Highs**: 0 significant highs.
    - The market struggled during the Great Depression. Recovery started in the early 1940s but remained below pre-crash levels.
- **New Lows**: 1 significant low.
    - The most significant low occurred on **July 8, 1932**, when the Dow dropped to **41.22**, marking the bottom of the Great Depression.

Major Events:

- **Stock Market Crash**: October 29, 1929 – Start of the Great Depression.
- **1932 Presidential Election**: November 8, 1932 – Franklin D. Roosevelt was elected President.
- **New Deal**: Launched on March 4, 1933, to combat the Great Depression.

---

[2] Data - www.dqydj.com/dow-jones-return-calculator/

- **Social Security Act**: Signed into law on August 14, 1935.
- **World War II**: September 1, 1939 – September 2, 1945 (U.S. entered after Pearl Harbor on December 7, 1941).

- **1944 Presidential Election**: November 7, 1944 – Franklin D. Roosevelt was re-elected for a 4th term.
- **End of World War II**: May 8, 1945 (VE Day in Europe), September 2, 1945 (VJ Day in Japan).
- **Roosevelt's Death**: April 12, 1945 – Franklin D. Roosevelt died; Harry S. Truman became President.
- **United Nations Established**: October 24, 1945.
- **First Baby Boomers are Born**: January 1, 1944.

Recessions and the Markets:

The Great Depression (1929-1933)

- **Duration**: August 1929 – March 1933 (43 months)
- **Stock Market Impact**:
    - The DJIA lost nearly 89% of its value between 1929 and 1932, marking the largest and most devastating market decline in U.S. history.

- The crash of 1929, starting with "Black Tuesday" on October 29, 1929, is considered the start of the Great Depression.

Recession of 1937-1938

- **Duration**: May 1937 – June 1938 (13 months)
- **Stock Market Impact**:
    - The Dow dropped nearly 50% between August 1937 and March 1938 following tight fiscal and monetary policy, including the tightening of the Federal Reserve.
    - This was a severe correction after the initial recovery from the Great Depression.

Recession of 1945

- **Duration**: February 1945 – October 1945 (8 months)
- **Stock Market Impact**:

- The stock market was flat during the recession as the economy transitioned from wartime to peacetime.
- Despite a short downturn, the DJIA rebounded with the post-war economic boom.

The stock market crash of 1929 was more than just a financial catastrophe; it was the beginning of the most severe economic downturn in modern history—the Great Depression. This period, which spanned from 1929 to the onset of World War II, transformed the U.S. economy and the global financial landscape.

The collapse of the stock market triggered widespread unemployment, bank failures, and social unrest, while the eventual involvement of the United States in World War II played a crucial role in reviving the economy. This chapter examines the causes and consequences of the Great Depression, the government's response through the New Deal, and the profound impact of World War II on the U.S. economy and stock market.

3.1 The Crash of 1929 and the Subsequent Market Collapse

The stock market crash of 1929 is often seen as the spark that ignited the Great Depression, but the roots of the economic collapse went much deeper. The speculative excesses of the 1920s had created an unsustainable bubble, and when that bubble burst, it revealed the underlying weaknesses in the American economy and financial system. The crash wiped out billions of dollars in wealth and shattered the confidence of investors, businesses, and consumers alike.

3.1.1 The Stock Market Crash of 1929

On October 24, 1929, known as Black Thursday, the first wave of panic hit Wall Street. Stock prices, which had been rising steadily throughout the 1920s, began to fall sharply, triggering a selling frenzy. Banks and investment firms attempted to intervene, buying up large amounts of stock to stabilize the market. However, their efforts were in vain, and the panic had spread across the country by the following week.

Black Tuesday, October 29, 1929, marked the final collapse. On that day, more than 16 million shares were traded, and stock prices plummeted to new lows. Investors who had borrowed money to buy stocks on margin were hit particularly hard, as they were forced to sell their holdings at a loss to meet margin calls. The result was a vicious cycle of selling that further depressed stock prices. By the end of the day, the stock market had lost nearly 12% of its value, and the U.S. economy was on the brink of collapse.

The psychological impact of the crash was profound. For many Americans, the stock market symbolized the promise of prosperity and wealth during the 1920s. The sudden and catastrophic collapse shattered that illusion, leading to widespread fear and uncertainty. Investors who had once believed in the inevitability of perpetual growth were now faced with the harsh reality that the market could fall as quickly as it had risen.

3.1.2 The Great Depression Unfolds

The stock market crash of 1929 did not cause the Great Depression by itself, but it played a central role in triggering the broader economic collapse that followed. As stock prices fell, banks that had lent money to investors and speculators found themselves in trouble. Many banks had invested heavily in the stock market, and when stock prices collapsed, so did their capital. This led to a wave of bank failures nationwide, further exacerbating the financial crisis.

With the banking system in disarray, businesses could not secure the loans they needed to operate, leading to widespread bankruptcies and layoffs. As businesses closed their doors and unemployment soared, consumer demand plummeted, creating a deflationary spiral. Prices for goods and services fell as businesses attempted to attract customers, but there was little money to spend with millions of Americans out of work. By 1933, the U.S. economy had reached its lowest point. Unemployment stood at nearly 25%, and millions of Americans were struggling to survive. Breadlines and soup kitchens became common sights in cities across the country, while rural areas faced widespread poverty and agricultural collapse. The Great Depression was not just an economic crisis but a social and humanitarian disaster that affected every aspect of American life.

The ripple effects of the Great Depression were felt around the world. As the U.S. economy contracted, global trade slowed, and many countries dependent on American imports and investment faced economic hardship. In Europe, the economic crisis contributed to political instability, setting the stage for the rise of authoritarian regimes in countries like Germany and Italy. The Great Depression, in many ways, reshaped the global political and economic order.

3.2 The New Deal and Government Interventions

Faced with the most severe economic crisis in American history, the U.S. government was forced to take unprecedented action to stabilize the economy and provide relief to its citizens. The election of Franklin D. Roosevelt in 1932 marked a turning point in the government's response to the Great Depression. Roosevelt's New Deal, a series of programs and reforms to stimulate economic recovery, fundamentally changed the relationship between the federal government and the American economy.

3.2.1 FDR and the New Deal Programs

When Franklin D. Roosevelt took office in March 1933, the country was in the depths of the Great Depression. The banking system had collapsed, unemployment was at an all-time high, and public confidence in the government was at a historic low. Roosevelt recognized that bold and decisive action was needed to restore confidence and jumpstart the economy. One of Roosevelt's first acts as president was to declare a national bank holiday, closing all banks for several days to prevent further withdrawals and bank runs. During this time, the government passed the Emergency Banking Act, which provided federal support to stabilize the banking system and allowed only solvent banks to reopen. This move helped restore public confidence in the banking system and marked the beginning of Roosevelt's efforts to address the crisis.

The New Deal consisted of various programs designed to provide relief, recovery, and reform. Some of the most notable programs included the Works Progress Administration (WPA), which provided jobs for millions of unemployed Americans, and the Civilian Conservation Corps (CCC), which employed young men to work on public projects such as building roads and planting trees. The Social Security Act passed in 1935, established a safety net for the elderly and unemployed, providing benefits to those who were most vulnerable during the Depression. In addition to providing relief to individuals, the New Deal also sought to reform the financial system to prevent future crises. The Glass-Steagall Act, passed in 1933, separated commercial and investment banking, a move that was intended to reduce the risks associated with speculative investments. The creation of the Securities and Exchange Commission (SEC) in 1934 provided oversight of the stock market, ensuring that companies provided accurate financial information to investors and that trading practices were fair and transparent.

Roosevelt's New Deal was not without its critics. Some argued that the government's economic intervention was too heavy-handed and that the programs were inefficient and wasteful. Others, particularly conservative business leaders, feared that the New Deal would lead to socialism and undermine the free market system. However, for millions of Americans who were struggling to survive during the Great Depression, the New Deal represented a lifeline, providing jobs, relief, and hope for the future.

3.2.2 The Role of Regulation

One of the key legacies of the New Deal was the establishment of a regulatory framework that would govern the financial markets for decades to come. The Great Depression exposed serious flaws in the American financial system, particularly the lack of oversight and regulation that had allowed speculative excesses to go unchecked. Roosevelt and his administration recognized that in order to restore confidence in the financial system, they needed to impose new rules and safeguards to protect investors and the broader economy.

The Glass-Steagall Act, which created a clear separation between commercial banking and investment banking, was one of the most significant regulatory reforms of the New Deal era. Before the act, many banks had engaged in speculative activities, using depositors' funds to invest in the stock market. When the market crashed, these banks could not meet their obligations, leading to widespread failures. By separating these two types of banking, the Glass-Steagall Act reduced the risk that a bank's failure could destabilize the broader financial system.

The creation of the SEC was another critical reform. Before the establishment of the SEC, the stock market was largely unregulated, and practices such as insider trading and stock price manipulation were common. The SEC was tasked with enforcing new rules requiring companies to provide investors accurate financial information, ensuring that the market operated with greater transparency and fairness.

These regulatory reforms helped restore confidence in the financial system and provided a foundation for more stable and sustainable economic growth in the years that followed. While the New Deal did not end the Great Depression on its own, it laid the groundwork for the eventual recovery and helped prevent future financial crises from reaching the same level of devastation.

3.3 The Impact of World War II on the Economy and the Market

While the New Deal helped mitigate some of the worst effects of the Great Depression, the outbreak of World War II ultimately brought the U.S. economy out of its long slump. The war effort spurred an unprecedented mobilization of resources, creating millions of jobs and stimulating industrial production on a massive scale. By the end of the war, the United States had transformed from a country mired in economic depression to the world's leading economic superpower.

3.3.1 The Economic Mobilization for War

When the United States entered World War II in 1941, the country was still grappling with the effects of the Great Depression. However, the war effort required a massive mobilization of resources, and the federal government played a central role in directing the economy to meet the demands of the conflict.

The government created new agencies, such as the War Production Board (WPB), to oversee the allocation of materials and the conversion of civilian industries to military production. Factories that had once produced consumer goods, such as cars and appliances, were retooled to produce tanks, airplanes, and weapons. This shift in production created jobs for millions of Americans and revitalized industries that had been struggling during the Depression.

The war effort also led to the creation of new financial instruments, such as war bonds. The government encouraged Americans to buy war bonds as a way to finance the conflict, and millions of citizens participated in the program. War bonds helped fund the war and provided a safe and stable investment for individuals, many of whom had lost faith in the stock market during the Great Depression.

3.3.2 The Stock Market During Wartime

The stock market's performance during World War II was relatively stable compared to the wild fluctuations of the 1920s and 1930s. While the economy was heavily focused on the war effort, industries that were involved in military production saw significant growth. Defense-related stocks, such as those of companies manufacturing airplanes, ships, and weapons, performed particularly well during the war years.

Despite the overall stability of the market, the war years were marked by a high level of government intervention in the economy. The government imposed price controls and rationing to prevent inflation and ensure that resources were allocated efficiently. While these measures were necessary for the war effort, they also limited the potential for growth in many sectors of the economy.

As the war ended, there were concerns that the U.S. economy would fall back into depression. The end of the war meant a reduction in government spending on military production, and millions of soldiers were returning home, creating fears of widespread unemployment. However, these fears proved to be largely unfounded, as the post-war economy experienced a boom driven by pent-up consumer demand and the government's investments in infrastructure and education.

3.3.3 Post-War Repercussions

The end of World War II marked the beginning of a new era for the U.S. economy. The GI Bill passed in 1944, provided returning veterans access to education and housing, helping create a more educated and prosperous workforce. The housing boom that followed the war led to the growth of suburban America, while consumer spending surged as Americans used their savings to purchase homes, cars, and appliances.

The post-war period also saw the emergence of the United States as the dominant global economic power. The war had left much of Europe and Asia in ruins, and the U.S. became the world's leading exporter and creditor. The Marshall Plan, which provided aid to help rebuild Europe, further solidified the U.S.'s role as the global economy leader.

The stock market, which had been relatively stable during the war years, began to rise again as investors regained confidence in the post-war economy. By the late 1940s, the U.S. economy was growing rapidly, and the stock market was once again seen as a source of wealth and prosperity.

Chapter 4
Post-War Prosperity (1947-1964)

Bull Market – Expansion

Dow Jones Industrial

January 1, 1947 - 177

December 31, 1964 – 874.13

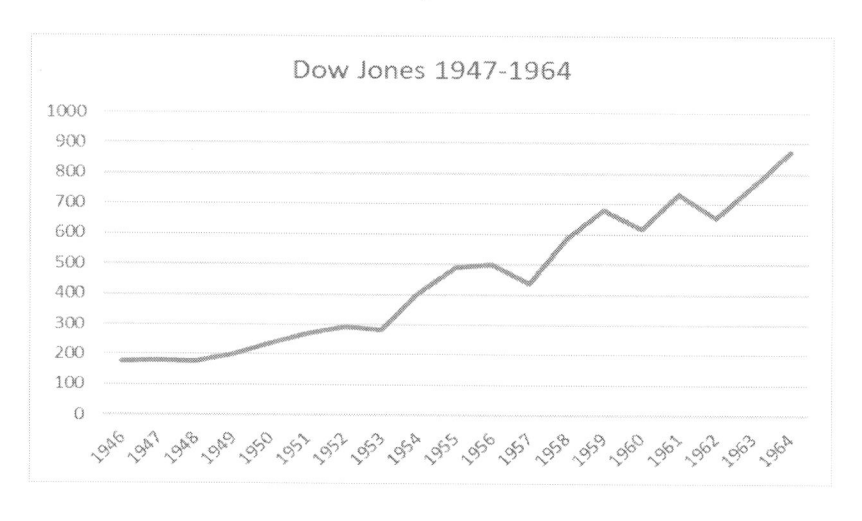

Dow Jones 1947-1964

Total Dow Jones Industrial Average Return – 392.181%

Annualized Dow Jones Industrial Average Return – 9.303%

Total DJIA Return (Dividends Reinvested) – 1080.385%

Annualized DJIA Return (Dividends Reinvested) – 14.771%[3]

- **New Highs**: 8 significant highs.
    - The Dow reached several new highs during this post-war period, including crossing **500** on **January 5, 1956**.
    - The Dow closed the period near **874.12** in **October 1964**.
- **New Lows**: 0 significant lows.
    - This period did not experience significant lows as the economy grew steadily.

Major Events:

- **Truman Doctrine**: March 12, 1947 – U.S. foreign policy aimed at containing communism.
- **Korean War**: June 25, 1950 – July 27, 1953.
- **1952 Presidential Election**: November 4, 1952 – Dwight D. Eisenhower was elected.

---

[3] Data - www.dqydj.com/dow-jones-return-calculator/

- **Sputnik Launched**: October 4, 1957 – Start of the Space Race.
- **First Televised Debate:** September 26, 1960 – JFK and Richard Nixon Debate.
- **1960 Presidential Election**: November 8, 1960 – John F. Kennedy was elected President.
- **Flash Crash of 1962**: May 28, 1962 – 1962, the Dow Jones was down 22.5% and down 5.7% on this day alone.
- **Cuban Missile Crisis**: October 16-28, 1962 – Standoff between the U.S. and the Soviet Union over missiles in Cuba.
- **Kennedy Assassination**: November 22, 1963 – President John F. Kennedy was assassinated; Lyndon B. Johnson became President.
- **Vietnam War**: August 2, 1964 (Gulf of Tonkin Incident) – U.S. involvement escalates, ending on April 30, 1975.
- **1964 Presidential Election**: November 3, 1964 – Lyndon B. Johnson was elected President.

Recession and the Markets:

Recession of 1949

- **Duration**: November 1948 – October 1949 (11 months)
- **Stock Market Impact**:
    - The Dow dropped roughly 16% during the recession.
    - The market rebounded rapidly once the economy returned to growth in 1949.

Recession of 1953

- **Duration**: July 1953 – May 1954 (10 months)
- **Stock Market Impact**:
    - The Dow fell around 10%, influenced by the end of the Korean War and monetary tightening.
    - The market rebounded quickly as the recession ended.

Recession of 1957-1958

- **Duration**: August 1957 – April 1958 (8 months)
- **Stock Market Impact**:
    - The DJIA fell approximately 15% during the recession as industrial production slowed.
    - Recovery was strong in late 1958 as consumer demand picked up.

Recession of 1960-1961

- **Duration**: April 1960 – February 1961 (10 months)
- **Stock Market Impact**:
    - The DJIA dropped around 13% in 1960.
    - The market saw a strong recovery during the early 1960s under President Kennedy.

The period following World War II marked one of the most prosperous eras in American economic history. From 1946 to 1963, the U.S. experienced rapid economic growth, technological innovation, and the rise of consumer culture.

This era, often referred to as the "Golden Age of Capitalism," was fueled by a combination of factors: the Marshall Plan's economic aid to Europe, the baby boomer generation, and the post-war technological advancements that revolutionized industries. The stock market, reflecting the buoyant mood of the country, entered a prolonged period of expansion, with corporate profits and investor optimism driving up stock prices. However, underlying this prosperity were challenges that would emerge later in the 20th century, as the economy began to shift toward new dynamics in labor, trade, and technological competition.

4.1 The Marshall Plan and the Recovery of Europe

After World War II, Europe was left in ruins. The war had decimated its infrastructure, industries, and economies, leaving the continent unable to recover on its own. The United States, which had emerged from the war as the dominant global economic power, recognized the need to aid Europe's reconstruction. This recognition was not just motivated by humanitarian concerns but also by the strategic interest of containing the spread of communism, which was gaining ground in the war-ravaged countries of Eastern Europe. Thus, the U.S. government enacted the Marshall Plan, a massive aid package designed to rebuild Europe's economies and stabilize the region politically.

4.1.1 The Origins and Objectives of the Marshall Plan

The Marshall Plan, named after Secretary of State George C. Marshall, was introduced in 1948 and provided over $13 billion (equivalent to more than $100 billion today) in economic assistance to European nations. The plan's primary goals were to rebuild war-torn Europe, revive European industry, and remove trade barriers to foster free-market economies. In addition, it aimed to curb the spread of communism by providing economic stability in Western Europe, a region vulnerable to political upheaval in the post-war years.

Marshall's vision for Europe was a continent rebuilt on democratic principles and economic cooperation. The plan was not just about immediate relief—it was also designed to create the conditions for long-term growth. As part of the Marshall Plan, the U.S. provided aid in the form of food, fuel, machinery, and raw materials. This helped European nations rebuild their industries, stabilize their currencies, and restore public confidence in their economies.

The Marshall Plan also had significant economic benefits for the United States. By helping Europe rebuild, the U.S. created new markets for its own goods and services. American companies, especially those in manufacturing and agriculture, found eager buyers in Europe, which boosted U.S. exports and contributed to the post-war economic boom. The Marshall Plan also laid the groundwork for greater economic cooperation between the U.S. and Europe, eventually leading to the creation of institutions such as the European Economic Community (EEC) and later the European Union.

4.1.2 Economic Revival in Europe

The economic impact of the Marshall Plan was profound. Within a few years of its implementation, European economies began to recover rapidly. Industrial output in Western Europe rose dramatically, and by the mid-1950s, the continent had largely rebuilt its infrastructure. Countries like France, West Germany, and Italy saw their industries modernized, their export markets revitalized, and their living standards improved.

In Germany, the Marshall Plan played a key role in the Wirtschaftswunder, or "economic miracle," as the country experienced unprecedented growth and industrial expansion. With American aid, German factories were rebuilt, and the country became a leading exporter of manufactured goods. The economic recovery in Germany was so strong that by the 1960s, it was competing with the U.S. in key industries such as automobile manufacturing and heavy machinery.

The recovery of Europe had a positive effect on the global economy as well. As European countries became more prosperous, they increased their imports from the United States, fueling demand for American goods. This helped drive economic growth in the U.S., creating jobs and increasing corporate profits. The post-war economic boom in the U.S. and Europe created a virtuous cycle of growth, trade, and investment that defined the global economy for much of the mid-20th century.

4.2 The Baby Boomer Generation and Consumer Spending

In the United States, the post-war period was marked by a demographic explosion. Between 1946 and 1964, the U.S. experienced a significant increase in birth rates, a phenomenon known as the "baby boom." This generation, born after World War II, would become one of the most influential demographic groups in U.S. history, shaping everything from economic policy to popular culture.

4.2.1 The Baby Boom Phenomenon

The baby boom was driven by a number of factors. The end of World War II brought millions of soldiers home, eager to start families and build new lives. The economic prosperity of the post-war years gave American families the financial security they needed to have children, buy homes, and invest in the future. Advances in medicine and healthcare also played a role, as infant mortality rates declined and life expectancy increased.

Between 1946 and 1964, more than 76 million babies were born in the United States, creating a massive new generation of consumers. This demographic shift had profound implications for the U.S. economy. As the baby boomers grew up, they fueled demand for a wide range of goods and services, from baby products and toys in their early years to cars, homes, and higher education as they entered adulthood. This surge in consumer demand drove economic growth and created new business opportunities.

4.2.2 The Rise of Consumer Culture

One of the defining characteristics of the post-war period was the rise of consumer culture. In the years following World War II, the U.S. economy shifted from one focused on production to one driven by consumption. American families, buoyed by rising incomes and increased access to credit, began purchasing goods at an unprecedented rate. The consumer goods that had been scarce during the war—cars, appliances, clothing—were now widely available, and the growing middle class was eager to buy them.

The automobile industry, which had played a key role in the industrial expansion of the 1920s, once again became a driving force in the post-war economy. With more disposable income, American families began purchasing cars in record numbers, and by the 1950s, car ownership had become a symbol of middle-class success. As millions of Americans moved from cities to newly built suburbs, the rise of suburbanization further fueled demand for automobiles. The construction of the Interstate Highway System, which began in 1956, provided the infrastructure needed to support this car-centric way of life.

In addition to cars, the post-war period saw a boom in the production and consumption of household appliances. Refrigerators, washing machines, televisions, and other modern conveniences became standard features in American homes. The introduction of consumer credit, including the rise of credit cards, made it easier for families to purchase these goods, even if they did not have the cash to pay for them upfront.

Advertising played a crucial role in promoting consumer culture. With the rise of television as a dominant medium, advertisers used mass media to create demand for products and shape public perceptions of what it meant to live the "good life." Companies spent millions of dollars on advertising campaigns that encouraged Americans to buy more, often appealing to their desires for status, convenience, and comfort.

This explosion in consumer spending had a transformative effect on the U.S. economy. Industries that produced consumer goods—such as automobiles, appliances, and electronics—experienced rapid growth, creating millions of jobs and driving corporate profits. The stock market, which had been relatively stable during the war years, entered a period of sustained growth as investors capitalized on the booming economy. Major corporations like General Motors, Ford, and General Electric became the blue-chip stocks of the era, offering consistent returns to shareholders.

4.3 Technological Innovations and the Rise of American Corporations

The post-war period was also a time of significant technological advancements, many of which were rooted in the innovations developed during World War II. These technological breakthroughs transformed industries and helped propel the United States to global economic dominance. At the same time, large American corporations, many of which had grown during the war, became even more powerful and influential in shaping the domestic and international economy.

4.3.1 Technological Milestones

One of the most important technological developments of the post-war era was the rise of television. While television had been invented before World War II, it wasn't until the late 1940s and early 1950s that it became a mass-market product. By the mid-1950s, more than half of American households owned a television set, and the medium quickly became a dominant force in American culture. Television revolutionized how Americans received information and entertainment, creating new opportunities for advertising and transforming the political landscape.

Another significant technological advancement of the post-war period was the development of computers. Initially developed during World War II for military purposes, computers began to find commercial applications in the 1950s. Companies like IBM pioneered the development of mainframe computers, which large corporations and government agencies used for tasks such as data processing and scientific research. While computers were still in their infancy during this period, their potential to revolutionize business and industry became increasingly apparent.

In addition to television and computers, other technological innovations helped drive economic growth during the post-war years. The expansion of the aerospace industry, fueled by the Cold War and the space race, created new opportunities for research and development. The invention of the transistor in 1947 revolutionized electronics, leading to the development of smaller and more efficient devices, including radios, televisions, and eventually computers.

4.3.2 The Ascendancy of American Corporations

As the U.S. economy grew, so did the power and influence of American corporations. Many of the largest companies of the post-war period had grown rapidly during World War II when the government relied on private industry to produce the materials needed for the war effort. These companies, including giants like General Motors, Ford, and U.S. Steel, emerged from the war as dominant players in the global economy.

American corporations played a central role in the domestic economy and expanded their reach internationally. As Europe and Asia rebuilt their economies in the aftermath of the war,

American companies moved in to capture new markets. The rise of multinational corporations, which operated in multiple countries and controlled vast resources, became a defining feature of the global economy in the post-war years.

The success of American corporations during this period was reflected in the stock market. The 1950s and early 1960s were a time of steady growth for the stock market as corporate profits rose and investors reaped the rewards. The Dow Jones Industrial Average, which had stagnated during the war years, more than doubled between 1949 and 1959. This period of sustained growth created wealth for millions of Americans, who increasingly saw the stock market as a reliable way to build financial security. While American corporations enjoyed unprecedented success during this period, there were also signs of emerging challenges. The rise of labor unions, which had gained strength during the war, led to increased demands for higher wages and better working conditions. At the same time, the growth of international competition, particularly from countries like Japan and West Germany, began to pressure American companies to innovate and become more efficient. These challenges would come to the forefront in the decades that followed as the U.S. economy faced new realities in the global marketplace.

4.4 The Seeds of Future Challenges

While the post-war period was a time of great prosperity, it also laid the groundwork for many economic and social challenges that would emerge in the latter half of the 20th century. The rise of consumer debt, the growing power of multinational corporations, and the increasing influence of labor unions were all trends that would shape the economic landscape in the decades to come.

One of the most significant challenges was the growing reliance on consumer credit. As Americans embraced the idea of living beyond their means, borrowing money to buy cars, homes, and other goods became increasingly common. While this fueled economic growth in the short term, it also created the potential for financial instability. The expansion of consumer credit would later contribute to economic crises such as the savings and loan crisis of the 1980s and the housing market crash of 2008. The rise of multinational corporations also had long-term implications for the U.S. economy. As

American companies expanded overseas operations, they became less dependent on the domestic market. This shift would lead to tensions in the decades to come as companies sought to maximize profits by outsourcing production to countries with lower labor costs. The decline of American manufacturing, which began in the 1970s, can be traced in part to the decisions made by corporations during the post-war period to prioritize international expansion.

Finally, the growing power of labor unions during the post-war years created a new dynamic in the American economy. Unions successfully negotiated higher wages and better benefits for workers, contributing to the rise of the middle class. However, these gains also put pressure on companies to increase productivity and cut costs. In the decades that followed, the relationship between labor and management would become increasingly contentious as globalization and technological change transformed the workplace.

In addition to these economic shifts, the post-war era marked the beginning of significant cultural and political changes. The election of John F. Kennedy in 1960 symbolized hope and change for many Americans. His youth and charisma resonated with a generation yearning for new leadership, and his presidency coincided with the burgeoning Civil Rights Movement, a growing counterculture, and an intensifying Cold War.

Kennedy's assassination on November 22, 1963, was a profound cultural and psychological shock to the nation. His death not only altered the political landscape but also intensified the cultural tensions already brewing in the country. For many Americans, it symbolized the end of post-war optimism and the beginning of a more uncertain and tumultuous time. While the stock market initially responded with shock and uncertainty, the economic fundamentals remained strong. Nonetheless, the assassination marked a turning point, as it highlighted the fragility of leadership and the complexity of the social and political challenges the country faced.

Kennedy's assassination became a national trauma that magnified emerging cultural divisions, and it contributed to the sense of instability that would define much of the 1960s. As the nation grappled with the loss, Americans also began to confront deeper questions about identity, values, and the country's future direction. The event catalyzed a shift in the national psyche, as it became clear that the prosperity of the post-war years could not insulate the nation from deeper social and political unrest.

While the economic growth of the late 1940s and 1950s continued into the early 1960s, the social and political unrest that followed Kennedy's assassination foreshadowed the volatility that would characterize the stock market and the nation in the years to come. The economic challenges born out of the rise of consumer debt, corporate expansion, and labor unrest were mirrored by cultural shifts, with Kennedy's assassination serving as a symbolic turning point in America's post-war narrative.

Chapter 5
The Vietnam War, Stagflation and Social Upheaval (1965-1981)

Bear Market – Contraction

Dow Jones Industrial

Flat or Neutral return

January 1, 1965 – 874.13

December 31, 1981 – 875[4]

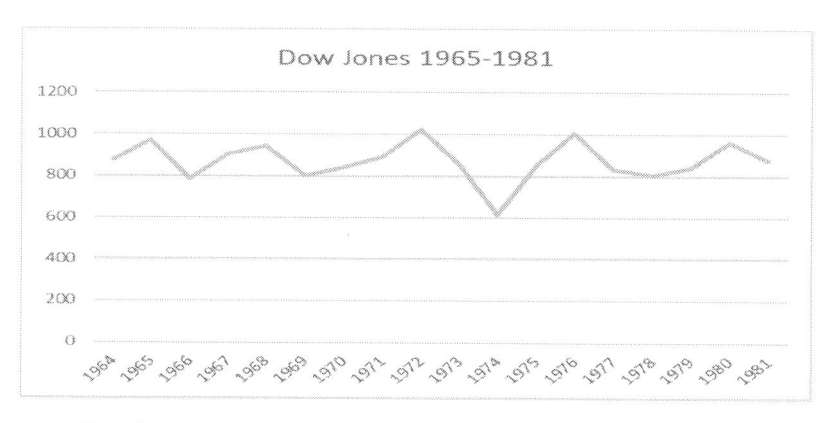

```
Dow Jones 1965-1981
```

Total Dow Jones Industrial Average Return - -1.305%

Annualized Dow Jones Industrial Average Return - -0.078%

---

[4] Data - www.dqydj.com/dow-jones-return-calculator/

Total DJIA Return (Dividends Reinvested) – 110.078%

Annualized DJIA Return (Dividends Reinvested) – 4.486%

- **New Highs**: 3 significant highs.
    - The Dow hit new highs, reaching **995** in **1966** and crossing **1,000** in **1981**.
- **New Lows**: 1 significant low.
    - A major low occurred during the **1974 recession**, with the Dow falling to **577.60**.

Major Events:

- **Assassination of Martin Luther King Jr.**: April 4, 1968.
- **Assassination of Robert F. Kennedy**: June 5, 1968.
- **Woodstock**: August 15, 1969.
- **Apollo 11 Moon Landing**: July 20, 1969 – First manned mission to land on the moon.
- **1972 Presidential Election**: November 7, 1972 – Richard Nixon was re-elected President.
- **Munich Games Massacre**: September 5, 1972.
- **1973 Oil Embargo**: 1973-1974.

- **Roe v. Wade**: January 22, 1973 – Supreme Court legalizes abortion.
- **Watergate Scandal**: June 17, 1972 – A break-in led to a major political scandal, resulting in Nixon's resignation.
- **Nixon Resigns**: August 8, 1974 – Richard Nixon resigned; **Gerald Ford becomes President.**
- **Vietnam War Ends**: April 30, 1975 – The fall of Saigon marked the end of the war.
- **1976 Presidential Election**: November 2, 1976 – Jimmy Carter was elected President.
- **Iran Hostage Crisis**: November 4, 1979 – January 20, 1981 – 52 Americans held hostage for 444 days.
- **1980 Presidential Election**: November 4, 1980 – Ronald Reagan was elected President.
- **Recession of 1980 – 1981**: Unemployment reaches 10%, inflation rampant, Fed Fund Rate reaches historical 20%.
- **Assassination Attempt on Reagan**: March 30, 1981 – Reagan survives being shot.

Recession and the Markets:

Recession of 1969-1970

- **Duration**: December 1969 – November 1970 (11 months)
- **Stock Market Impact**:
  - The Dow dropped by around 30% from late 1968 to mid-1970 due to tight monetary policy and rising inflation.
  - Recovery was slow, and the market continued to struggle into the mid-1970s.

1973-1975 Recession

- **Duration**: November 1973 – March 1975 (16 months).
- **Stock Market Impact**:
  - The DJIA fell about 45% from January 1973 to December 1974, largely due to the 1973 oil crisis and stagflation.
  - The market began to recover after March 1975, with economic growth resuming.

1980 Recession

- **Duration**: January 1980 – July 1980 (6 months)
- **Stock Market Impact**:
    - The Dow dropped around 17% during the short recession.
    - The recovery was brief, as the economy entered another recession shortly after.

1981 Recession

- **Duration**: July 1981 – November 1982 (16 months)
- **Stock Market Impact**:
    - The DJIA lost nearly 24% from April 1981 to August 1982, largely due to high interest rates set by the Federal Reserve to combat inflation.
    - A strong bull market began in August 1982 as inflation was brought under control.

The period between 1964 and 1981 was marked by dramatic shifts in the U.S. economy and stock market. This era witnessed the costly Vietnam War, rising inflation, and the unprecedented phenomenon of stagflation—a situation in which high inflation occurred simultaneously with stagnant economic growth.

As the post-war prosperity of the 1950s and early 1960s faded, the U.S. economy faced growing challenges, including increased government spending on the war, rising oil prices, and a global economic realignment. In this chapter, we will explore the escalation of the Vietnam War to the oil crises of the 1970s, stagflation, and the Watergate scandal and how the Federal Reserve's policies shaped the stock market during this tumultuous period.

Additionally, the assassinations of Martin Luther King Jr. and Robert Kennedy, along with landmark civil rights legislation, left lasting imprints on the nation.

5.1 The Impact of the Vietnam War on the Economy

The Vietnam War, which escalated significantly under President Lyndon B. Johnson's administration in the mid-1960s, had profound economic consequences for the United States. While the war did not lead to the kind of economic boom experienced during World War II, it placed enormous pressure on government spending, contributed to rising inflation, and led to significant public unrest. The economic consequences of the war were felt both in the stock market and the broader economy, setting the stage for the difficult economic conditions of the 1970s.

5.1.1 War Spending and Fiscal Policy

One of the most immediate effects of the Vietnam War was the sharp increase in government spending. Defense spending soared as the U.S. military escalated its involvement in Southeast Asia. By the late 1960s, the U.S. was spending billions of dollars annually to support the war effort, a significant increase from the relatively low defense spending levels of the early post-war period. This surge in government spending contributed to growing budget deficits, as the federal government borrowed heavily to finance the war.

Unlike during World War II, when the U.S. government raised taxes to help fund the war effort, the Vietnam War was largely financed through borrowing. President Johnson's decision to avoid raising taxes, partly due to his desire to fund the domestic

Great Society programs, led to a significant increase in the national debt. The combination of high government spending on the war and domestic programs put tremendous pressure on the federal budget, leading to mounting deficits.

The impact of this fiscal policy was felt in the broader economy, as the increased borrowing by the federal government led to higher interest rates and inflation. As the government issued more bonds to finance the war, the supply of money in the economy increased, leading to upward pressure on prices. This inflationary pressure would become one of the defining features of the 1970s economy.

5.1.2 Social Unrest and the Anti-War Movement

The economic impact of the Vietnam War was not limited to inflation and government deficits. The war also contributed to widespread social unrest as the American public grew increasingly disillusioned with the conflict. By the late 1960s, anti-war protests had become a regular feature of American life, with students, civil rights activists, and other groups calling for an end to the war.

The social unrest created by the anti-war movement had economic consequences as well. Businesses were affected by strikes, protests, and disruptions, leading to losses in productivity. Moreover, the growing polarization of American society—fueled by the war, the civil rights movement, and the counterculture—made it more difficult for the government to implement coherent economic policies. The unrest contributed to a sense of uncertainty in the stock market, as investors worried about the stability of the political and social environment.

5.1.3 Inflationary Pressures

One of the most significant economic legacies of the Vietnam War was the inflation that accelerated in the late 1960s and continued throughout the 1970s. The combination of high government spending, increased borrowing, and rising wages contributed to a general price increase across the economy. By the early 1970s, inflation had become a major concern for policymakers, as it eroded the purchasing power of consumers and contributed to growing discontent among the public. Inflation was exacerbated by the decision in 1971 to abandon the gold standard, which had previously linked the value of the

U.S. dollar to a fixed quantity of gold. This move, known as the "Nixon shock," was intended to give the government greater flexibility in managing the economy but also removed a key constraint on monetary policy. With the dollar no longer tied to gold, the Federal Reserve had more freedom to increase the money supply, which contributed to further inflation.

As inflation rose, businesses faced higher costs for raw materials, labor, and other inputs, leading to a decline in profitability. Consumers, in turn, were squeezed by rising prices, particularly for essential goods such as food and fuel. This combination of rising costs and declining real incomes created a sense of economic anxiety, which would become even more pronounced in the years ahead.

5.2 Social and Political Upheaval: The Assassinations, Rights and Resignation

5.2.1 The Voting Rights Act of 1965

Amidst the turbulence of the 1960s, the passage of the Voting Rights Act in 1965 was a landmark victory for civil rights. Signed into law by President Lyndon B. Johnson, the Act sought to eliminate the discriminatory practices that had long prevented African Americans from exercising their right to vote, particularly in the South.

By banning literacy tests, poll taxes, and other forms of voter suppression, the Voting Rights Act dramatically increased African American voter participation. This reshaped the political landscape of the United States and marked a critical moment in the fight for racial equality.

5.2.2 Martin Luther King Jr. (1929-1968)

On April 4, 1968, the United States was shaken to its core when Martin Luther King Jr., one of the most prominent leaders of the civil rights movement and a global icon for non-violent resistance, was assassinated in Memphis, Tennessee. King had been in Memphis to support a strike by sanitation workers, reinforcing his deep belief in the fight against economic injustice in addition to racial inequality. His murder sent shockwaves across the nation, igniting widespread riots in more than 100 cities, including major unrest in Washington, D.C., Chicago, and Baltimore. These violent protests reflected the pent-up frustration of Black Americans, whose hopes for equality and justice had been championed by King but were yet to be fully realized.

Throughout his career, King played an instrumental role in securing landmark legislative victories for civil rights, such as the Civil Rights Act of 1964 and the Voting Rights Act of 1965. These laws aimed to dismantle systemic racial segregation and ensure voting rights for African Americans, making them key milestones in the struggle for equality. King's philosophy of non-violent protest, inspired by Mahatma Gandhi, helped galvanize peaceful resistance to oppression and inspired countless other social justice movements worldwide.

However, King's assassination laid bare the racial tensions still deeply embedded in American society. His death left a profound void in the leadership of the civil rights movement, one that was difficult to fill as activists debated the future direction of the cause—whether to continue with non-violence or adopt more radical measures. The social unrest following King's death, coupled with existing economic challenges like rising inflation and unemployment, added to the sense of national instability. It marked a turning point in American history, a period of reflection on the profound inequalities that still plagued the country, and ushered in an era of uncertainty both politically and economically.

5.2.3 Robert F. Kennedy (1925-1968)

Just two months after the tragic assassination of Martin Luther King Jr., the United States was once again plunged into mourning with the murder of Senator Robert F. Kennedy. On June 5, 1968, after delivering a victory speech at the Ambassador Hotel in Los Angeles, Kennedy was shot by an assassin as he was campaigning for the Democratic nomination for President of the United States. Known affectionately as "Bobby" to the public, Robert F. Kennedy was a passionate advocate for civil rights, an ardent opponent of racial injustice, and a vocal critic of the Vietnam War—a conflict that had bitterly divided the nation.

Robert Kennedy had become a beacon of hope for many Americans, particularly those disillusioned by the political establishment and the ongoing war. His vision for America was one of inclusion, equality, and peace, much like that of his late brother, President John F. Kennedy, who had been assassinated five years earlier in 1963. For many, Robert's presidential campaign signified the potential for a new chapter in American politics—a move towards unity and healing during one of the most turbulent times in U.S. history.

His assassination deepened the national trauma and intensified the feelings of despair among Americans. The back-to-back murders of two of the most significant voices for change—King and Kennedy—left the country grappling with a sense of hopelessness, further exacerbating the societal tensions of the time. With Kennedy's death, the American public's trust in its political system reached a nadir, as the nation was still reeling from widespread protests, anti-war demonstrations, and civil unrest. Many viewed his assassination as the final blow to the idealism and optimism of the 1960s, marking a tragic and somber turning point in a year already fraught with violence and upheaval.

The combined loss of King and Kennedy in such a short period not only amplified the sense of national disillusionment but also highlighted the deep divisions within American society—divisions over race, war, and the direction of the nation's future. For years to come, their deaths would serve as painful reminders of the struggles America faced in trying to reconcile its ideals with its realities.

5.2.4 The Resignation of President Nixon

The Watergate scandal, which erupted in the early 1970s, culminated in the resignation of President Richard Nixon on August 8, 1974—the first time in American history that a sitting president resigned. The scandal, which began with a break-in at the Democratic National Committee headquarters, spiraled into a broader investigation into abuses of power and led to the eventual discovery of Nixon's efforts to obstruct justice. Nixon's resignation further eroded public trust in government institutions, which had already been shaken by the Vietnam War and social unrest. Watergate led to significant political reforms aimed at increasing transparency, but the damage to public confidence was long-lasting. The political instability and the lingering economic challenges of the 1970s made this a particularly difficult time for the U.S.

5.3 The Oil Crisis and Stagflation

The 1970s are often remembered as a decade of economic turmoil, and one of the defining events of this period was the oil crisis of 1973. The crisis, triggered by a decision by the Organization of the Petroleum Exporting Countries (OPEC) to cut oil production and raise prices, sent shockwaves through the global economy. The U.S., which had become increasingly dependent on foreign oil, was particularly hard hit, and the crisis contributed to the emergence of stagflation—a period of high inflation combined with stagnant economic growth.

5.3.1 The Oil Embargo of 1973

A combination of geopolitical and economic factors precipitated the oil crisis of 1973. In October of that year, OPEC, led by Saudi Arabia, announced an oil embargo in response to U.S. support for Israel during the Yom Kippur War. The embargo led to a sharp reduction in the global oil supply, causing prices to skyrocket. Within months, the price of oil had quadrupled, and the effects were felt throughout the global economy.

For the U.S., the oil crisis exposed the country's vulnerability to disruptions in the global energy market. As oil prices soared, the cost of gasoline, heating oil, and other petroleum products rose dramatically. Consumers were faced with long lines at gas stations, and businesses saw their energy costs increase sharply. The crisis also contributed to rising inflation, as higher energy costs were passed on to consumers through higher prices for goods and services.

The oil embargo had far-reaching consequences for the U.S. economy. The sharp increase in energy prices contributed to a slow economic growth as businesses and consumers cut back on spending in response to rising costs. At the same time, inflation continued to rise, creating a situation in which prices increased even as economic activity stagnated. This combination of inflation and stagnant growth—stagflation—was a new and troubling phenomenon for policymakers, who struggled to find solutions to the crisis.

5.3.2 Stagflation Takes Hold

Stagflation presented a unique challenge for economists and policymakers because it defied traditional economic theories. According to the Phillips curve, which economists had widely accepted in the post-war period, there was supposed to be a trade-off between inflation and unemployment: when inflation was high, unemployment was low, and vice versa. However, stagflation upended this relationship, as inflation and unemployment rose simultaneously.

The causes of stagflation were complex and multifaceted. In addition to the oil crisis, other factors contributed to the economic malaise of the 1970s. The Vietnam War had left the U.S. with large budget deficits, and the decision to abandon the gold standard had created uncertainty in global financial markets. Meanwhile, productivity growth, which had fueled economic expansion in the post-war years, began to slow, leading to a decline in real wages for many workers.

As inflation continued to rise, the Federal Reserve faced difficult choices. On the one hand, raising interest rates could help reduce inflation by curbing the money supply. On the other hand, higher interest rates could also lead to slower economic growth and higher unemployment.

In the 1970s, the Fed initially opted for a more accommodative monetary policy, keeping interest rates relatively low to stimulate economic growth. However, this approach only exacerbated inflation, leading to a vicious cycle of rising prices and stagnant growth.

5.3.3 The Impact on the Stock Market

The oil crisis and the subsequent stagflation profoundly impacted the stock market. During the early 1970s, stock prices had risen steadily, fueled by investor optimism and the post-war economic boom. However, the combination of rising inflation, high interest rates, and stagnant economic growth took a toll on investor confidence. The Dow Jones Industrial Average, which had peaked in 1973, entered a prolonged period of decline, losing nearly 45% of its value by the mid-1970s.

Investors faced a difficult environment, as stocks and bonds performed poorly during this period. Inflation eroded the real value of fixed-income investments while rising interest rates made it more expensive for companies to borrow money, leading to lower corporate profits and declining stock prices. The stock market, a reliable source of wealth generation in the post-war years, became increasingly volatile, and many investors sought refuge in alternative assets such as gold and real estate. The 1970s also saw a decline in investor participation in the stock market as many Americans became disillusioned with Wall Street. The scandals of the early 1970s, including the collapse of the Penn Central Railroad and the bankruptcy of several large brokerage firms, eroded public trust in the financial markets. At the same time, the economic uncertainty of the decade led many investors to adopt a more cautious approach, focusing on preserving capital rather than seeking high returns.

5.4 The Rise of Interest Rates and Federal Reserve Policies

As the 1970s drew to a close, inflation remained one of the most pressing issues facing the U.S. economy. The Federal Reserve, under the leadership of Paul Volcker, adopted a new approach to tackling inflation, one that would have far-reaching consequences for the stock market and the broader economy. Volcker's decision to raise interest rates to historically high levels helped bring inflation under control but also triggered a painful recession in the early 1980s.

5.4.1 The Volcker Shock

When Paul Volcker became chairman of the Federal Reserve in 1979, inflation was running at nearly 14%, and the economy was still struggling with the effects of stagflation. Volcker believed that the only way to bring inflation under control was to implement a series of aggressive interest rate hikes, known as the "Volcker shock." Under Volcker's leadership, the Federal Reserve raised the federal funds rate to nearly 20%, a level that had not been seen in decades.

Volcker's strategy was based on the belief that high interest rates would reduce inflation by curbing the money supply and reducing demand for goods and services. By making borrowing more expensive, the Fed hoped to cool off the economy and bring inflation down to more manageable levels. However, the short-term effects of the Volcker shock were severe. The sharp increase in interest rates led to a recession in the early 1980s, with unemployment reaching double digits and many businesses struggling to survive.

5.4.2 The Stock Market During the Volcker Era

The Volcker shock profoundly impacted the stock market, which had already been struggling throughout the 1970s. The high interest rates implemented by the Federal Reserve made it more expensive for companies to borrow money, leading to lower corporate profits and declining stock prices. At the same time, the high cost of borrowing also reduced consumer spending, further weakening the economy.

Despite the short-term pain caused by the Volcker shock, the strategy ultimately succeeded in bringing inflation under control. By the mid-1980s, inflation had fallen to less than 4%, and the U.S. economy began to recover. The stock market, which had languished for much of the 1970s, entered a period of sustained growth, setting the stage for the bull market of the 1980s and 1990s.

Volcker's policies were controversial then, as the high interest rates caused significant economic pain for many Americans. However, in retrospect, his decision to tackle inflation head-on is widely regarded as one of the most important factors in restoring stability to the U.S. economy. The lessons of the Volcker era continue to resonate today as policymakers grapple with the challenges of balancing inflation, growth, and interest rates.

5.5 The Transition to Reaganomics

The economic turmoil of the 1970s set the stage for a new era in U.S. economic policy. The election of Ronald Reagan in

1980 marked a significant shift in the government's approach to managing the economy, with a focus on reducing taxes, deregulation, and encouraging private sector growth. Reaganomics, as this new approach came to be known, would reshape the U.S. economy in the 1980s and beyond.

Reagan's economic policies were based on the principles of supply-side economics, which held that reducing taxes and government intervention would lead to increased investment, job creation, and economic growth. One of Reagan's first acts as president was to implement a series of tax cuts, including a reduction in the top marginal tax rate from 70% to 50%. These tax cuts, deregulation, and a more business-friendly environment helped stimulate economic growth in the 1980s.

At the same time, Reagan's administration pursued policies aimed at reducing inflation, including continued support for the high interest rates implemented by the Federal Reserve under Volcker. While these policies led to a temporary recession in the early 1980s, the economy rebounded strongly in the latter part of the decade, with the stock market entering one of the longest bull markets in U.S. history.

Chapter 6
Reaganomics and the Bull Market (1982-1999)

Bull Market – Expansion

Dow Jones Industrial

January 1, 1982 - 875

December 31, 1999 – 11497.12[5]

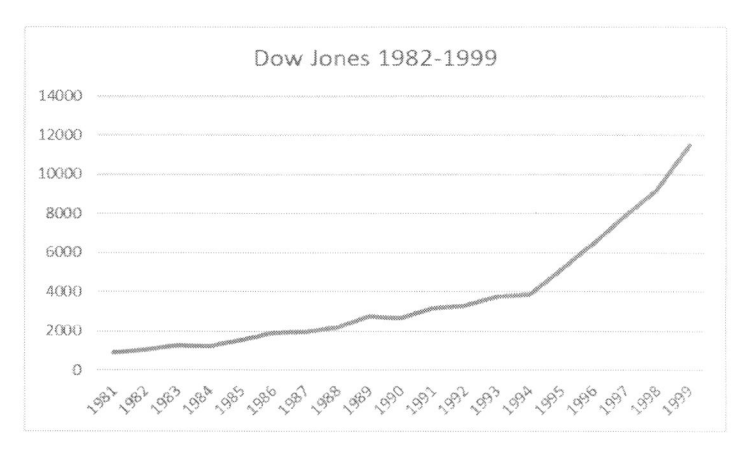

Dow Jones 1982-1999

Total Dow Jones Industrial Average Return – 1218.626%.

---

[5] Data - www.dqydj.com/dow-jones-return-calculator/

Annualized Dow Jones Industrial Average Return – 15.483%.

Total DJIA Return (Dividends Reinvested) – 2330.953%.

Annualized DJIA Return (Dividends Reinvested) – 19.494%.

- **New Highs**: 15 significant highs.
    - The Dow hit several milestones, including surpassing **2,000** in **1987** and reaching **11,497** in **1999**.
- **New Lows**: 1 significant low.
    - **Black Monday** on **October 19, 1987,** saw a 22.6% drop, with the Dow falling to **1,738.74**.

Major Events:

- **Space Shuttle Challenger Explodes**: April 25, 1986
- **Chernobyl Nuclear Plant** – April 26, 1986
- **Black Monday Stock Market Crash**: October 19, 1987 – Dow Jones Industrial Average drops by 22.6%.
- **1988 Presidential Election**: November 8, 1988 – George H. W. Bush was elected President.
- **Berlin Wall Falls**: November 9, 1989.

- **Gulf War**: August 2, 1990 – February 28, 1991 – U.S. leads a coalition to expel Iraq from Kuwait.
- **1992 Presidential Election**: November 3, 1992 – Bill Clinton was elected President.
- **Oklahoma City Bombing**: April 19, 1995 – Domestic terrorist attack kills 168 people.
- **Clinton Impeachment Trial**: December 19, 1998 – February 12, 1999 – Clinton becomes only the second president to be impeached. Later to be acquitted by the Senate.
- **Columbine High School Massacre**: April 20, 1999.

Recession and the Markets:

Early 1990s Recession

- **Duration**: July 1990 – March 1991 (8 months)
- **Stock Market Impact**:
    - The Dow fell around 18% during the recession, as the Gulf War and the savings and loan crisis weighed on the economy.
    - The market began a long recovery starting in 1991, continuing throughout the 1990s.

The period between 1982 and 1999 marked one of U.S. history's most significant economic transformations. The early 1980s were a time of economic recession, sky-high interest rates, and lingering stagflation. However, by the end of the 1990s, the U.S. was experiencing one of the longest and most prosperous bull markets in its history, driven by technological innovation, deregulation, and a shift in economic policy under President Ronald Reagan. This chapter will explore the key factors that shaped this period, from the rise of Reaganomics and supply-side economics to the explosive growth of the technology sector in the 1990s. The chapter will also examine the stock market's record-setting growth, the effects of globalization, and the seeds of volatility that would eventually lead to the Dot-Com Bust in 2000.

6.1 The Reagan Presidency and Supply-Side Economics

Ronald Reagan's election to the presidency in 1980 came when the U.S. economy was still reeling from the effects of stagflation, high unemployment, and rising inflation. Reagan's approach to the economy, known as "Reaganomics," was a radical departure from the policies of previous administrations. At the core of Reaganomics was the belief in supply-side economics, which posited that cutting taxes, reducing regulation, and encouraging investment would spur economic growth, increase employment, and ultimately benefit all sectors of society.

6.1.1 The Four Pillars of Reaganomics

Reaganomics rested on four key pillars: tax cuts, deregulation, controlling government spending, and tightening the money supply. These policies were designed to reduce the federal government's role in the economy and encourage private sector growth.

The most visible and immediate of these policies was Reagan's tax cuts. In 1981, the Economic Recovery Tax Act (ERTA) was passed, reducing the top marginal tax rate from 70% to 50%. Reagan argued that by cutting taxes, particularly for high-income earners and corporations, the government would stimulate investment and entrepreneurship, leading to greater economic growth. The theory was that the benefits of this growth would "trickle down" to all segments of society, creating jobs and increasing wages.

Deregulation was another central tenet of Reaganomics. The Reagan administration worked to reduce regulations in industries such as finance, telecommunications, energy, and transportation. By rolling back regulations, the government aimed to free businesses from bureaucratic constraints and encourage innovation and competition.

One of the most significant deregulatory moves was dismantling the Glass-Steagall Act, which had separated commercial and investment banking since the Great Depression. This decision would later have profound consequences for the financial industry. Controlling government spending was a more complicated challenge for Reagan. While he was committed to reducing the size of government and cutting social welfare programs, military spending increased significantly during his presidency. The Reagan administration's defense budget expanded dramatically as part of its efforts to win the Cold War, contributing to rising budget deficits.

Finally, Reagan supported the Federal Reserve's efforts under Chairman Paul Volcker to control inflation by tightening the money supply and maintaining high interest rates. This initially led to a deep recession in the early 1980s, but it also succeeded in bringing inflation under control, setting the stage for the economic recovery that followed.

6.1.2 The Impact of Tax Cuts and Deregulation

The immediate effects of Reagan's tax cuts and deregulatory policies were mixed. The economy experienced a sharp recession in 1981-1982, as the Federal Reserve's high interest rates and tight monetary policies led to a contraction in economic activity. Unemployment soared to over 10%, and the stock market, still struggling from the downturns of the 1970s, remained volatile.

However, by 1983, the U.S. economy began to rebound. Inflation, a persistent problem throughout the 1970s, finally came under control, and the combination of tax cuts and deregulation helped spur investment and economic growth. Corporate profits began to rise, and the stock market entered a period of sustained expansion. Reagan's supporters pointed to the economic recovery as proof that supply-side economics was working, while critics argued that the benefits of the recovery were disproportionately concentrated among the wealthy.

The stock market's performance was one of the most visible signs of the recovery. In August 1982, the Dow Jones Industrial Average (DJIA) was hovering around 800 points. By 1987, the DJIA had more than doubled, reaching over 2,700 points before the infamous Black Monday crash of October 19, 1987, when the market lost more than 20% of its value in a single day. Despite this crash, the stock market quickly recovered, and the bull market continued through the remainder of the 1980s and 1990s.

6.2 The Bull Market of the 1980s and 1990s

The stock market's performance between 1982 and 1999 is often referred to as one of the longest and most sustained bull markets in U.S. history. Fueled by economic growth, technological advancements, and a wave of corporate mergers and acquisitions, the market soared to new heights during this period. Investors, buoyed by rising corporate profits and the deregulation of the financial sector, poured money into stocks, leading to significant wealth creation.

6.2.1 Corporate Mergers and Takeovers

One of the defining features of the 1980s bull market was the wave of corporate mergers, takeovers, and leveraged buyouts (LBOs) that swept through the financial world. Companies sought to expand through acquisitions, often using borrowed money to finance their takeovers. This era of mergers and acquisitions (M&A) was partly driven by deregulation, which allowed companies greater freedom to engage in corporate restructuring.

Investment banks and private equity firms, such as Kohlberg Kravis Roberts (KKR), became key players in the M&A boom, using leveraged buyouts to acquire control of companies. One of the most famous LBOs of the 1980s was KKR's acquisition of RJR Nabisco in 1988, a deal worth $25 billion that became a symbol of the excesses of the decade. These takeovers often involved cutting costs, laying off workers, and restructuring companies to increase profitability.

The M&A boom helped drive stock prices higher as investors speculated on potential takeover targets and the profits that could be generated through corporate restructuring. However, the rise of leveraged buyouts also raised concerns about corporate debt levels and the long-term sustainability of the companies involved. By the late 1980s, many of the companies that had been acquired in LBOs were struggling with high levels of debt, leading to fears of a potential financial crisis.

6.2.2 Black Monday: The Crash of 1987

On October 19, 1987, the stock market experienced its largest one-day percentage decline in history, a day that became known as Black Monday. The DJIA plummeted by 22.6%, erasing billions of dollars in wealth in hours. The cause of the crash was not entirely clear at the time. However, many analysts pointed to a combination of factors, including computerized trading algorithms, rising interest rates, and concerns about inflation. Despite the severity of the crash, the market rebounded relatively quickly.

By the end of 1987, the DJIA had recovered much of its losses, and the economy continued to grow. Black Monday was a stark reminder of the volatility that can occur in financial markets, but it did not derail the broader bull market that would continue into the 1990s.

6.3 The Technology Boom of the 1990s

While the 1980s were marked by deregulation and corporate mergers, the 1990s were defined by the rise of the technology sector and the advent of the Internet. The tech boom of the 1990s was driven by a combination of factors, including advances in computing, the proliferation of personal computers, and the commercialization of the Internet. This period saw the rise of Silicon Valley as a global hub for innovation and the creation of some of the most valuable companies in the world.

6.3.1 The Rise of Silicon Valley and the Internet

The seeds of the technology boom were planted in the 1970s and 1980s with the development of microprocessors, personal computers, and the early internet. However, it wasn't until the 1990s that these technologies began to transform the global economy. Companies like Microsoft, Intel, and Apple became household names as personal computers became essential to business and daily life.

The commercialization of the internet in the mid-1990s was a game-changer for the technology sector. In 1993, the launch of the Mosaic web browser made the Internet accessible to the general public, and by the late 1990s, the Internet was transforming industries from media to retail. The rise of e-commerce companies like Amazon, which was founded in 1994, and the rapid growth of internet service providers created new opportunities for investors and entrepreneurs. Silicon Valley became the epicenter of the tech boom, attracting venture capital and talent from around the world. The region's culture of innovation and risk-taking led to the creation of startups that would revolutionize industries. By the late 1990s, companies like Yahoo!, Netscape, and AOL were at the forefront of the internet revolution, with their stock prices soaring as investors bet on the future of the digital economy.

6.3.2 The Dot-Com Bubble

The stock market's enthusiasm for technology stocks reached a fever pitch in the late 1990s as investors poured money into internet-based companies, many of which had little or no earnings. The "dot-com bubble," as it came to be known, was characterized by the rapid rise in the stock prices of internet companies, often driven by speculative fervor rather than solid financial performance.

Initial public offerings (IPOs) of tech companies became commonplace, with investors eager to get in on the ground floor of the next big internet success story. In many cases, these companies were valued not based on their current revenues or profits but on their potential to dominate emerging markets in the future. As a result, stock prices for tech companies skyrocketed, with the NASDAQ Composite index, which was heavily weighted toward technology stocks, rising more than 500% between 1995 and 2000.

However, by the end of the decade, it became clear that many of these companies were overvalued. As interest rates began to rise in the late 1990s and as investors grew increasingly concerned about the sustainability of the tech boom, the stock market began to falter. In 2000, the dot-com bubble would burst, wiping out billions of dollars in market value and leading to a sharp decline in the stock prices of many tech companies.

6.4 The Effects of Globalization and Trade

The acceleration of globalization and the liberalization of international trade also marked the 1980s and 1990s. As the U.S. economy grew, American companies increasingly looked to expand their operations overseas, taking advantage of lower labor costs and new markets for their products. At the same time, trade agreements like the North American Free Trade Agreement (NAFTA) and the World Trade Organization (WTO) opened up new opportunities for international commerce.

6.4.1 NAFTA and the WTO

One of the most significant trade agreements of the 1990s was NAFTA, which was signed by the U.S., Canada, and Mexico in 1994. NAFTA aimed to eliminate trade barriers between the three countries, creating a free trade zone that would allow for the more efficient movement of goods, services, and capital. Supporters of NAFTA argued that the agreement would boost economic growth by increasing exports and lowering costs for consumers.

At the same time, the creation of the WTO in 1995 marked a major step toward the liberalization of global trade. The WTO replaced the General Agreement on Tariffs and Trade (GATT) and established a formal framework for resolving trade disputes between countries. The U.S. played a leading role in shaping the WTO, with the goal of expanding global markets for American goods and services.

6.4.2 The Impact of Globalization on the Stock Market

The globalization of the U.S. economy had a profound impact on the stock market during the 1980s and 1990s. As American companies expanded overseas operations, they became less dependent on the domestic market, leading to increased profitability and higher stock prices. Multinational corporations like Coca-Cola, McDonald's, and General Electric became global giants, with operations in dozens of countries worldwide.

At the same time, globalization introduced new risks and challenges. The increased integration of the global economy made the U.S. more vulnerable to economic shocks from abroad, such as the Asian financial crisis of 1997. The crisis, which began in Thailand and spread to other Asian economies, led to a sharp decline in global stock markets and raised concerns about the stability of the international financial system. While the U.S. was relatively insulated from the direct effects of the crisis, it served as a reminder of the interconnectedness of the global economy.

6.5 The Seeds of the Dot-Com Bust

As the 1990s ended, the U.S. economy and stock market were riding high on the waves of technological innovation and globalization. The NASDAQ, driven by the tech boom, reached unprecedented levels, and investor enthusiasm for internet stocks seemed boundless. However, there were growing concerns beneath the surface that the market had become overvalued and that the tech bubble was unsustainable.

The seeds of the dot-com bust were sown in the late 1990s, as companies with little or no earnings were valued at billions of dollars based on speculative projections. Many tech companies had rushed to go public, raising capital through IPOs without a clear path to profitability. As interest rates began to rise in the late 1990s and as investors started to question the valuations of these companies, the stock market began to falter.

In March 2000, the NASDAQ peaked at over 5,000 points before beginning a sharp decline that would wipe out much of the market's gains from the previous five years. By 2002, the

NASDAQ had lost more than 75% of its value, and many of the internet companies that had been hailed as the future of the economy were bankrupt or struggling to survive.

The dot-com bust was a stark reminder of the dangers of speculative bubbles and the importance of sound financial fundamentals. While the stock market had experienced extraordinary growth during the 1980s and 1990s, the bust of 2000 marked the end of an era and set the stage for the economic challenges of the early 21st century.

Chapter 7
The Dot-Com Bust, 9/11 and the Great Recession (2000-2017)

Bear Market – Contraction

Dow Jones Industrial

January 1, 2000 - 11497.12

December 31, 2017 – 24719.22[6]

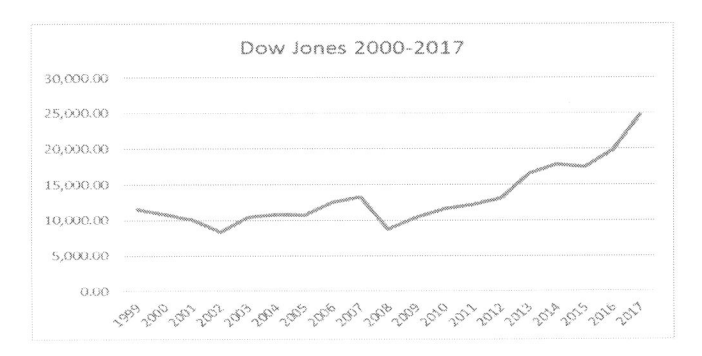

Dow Jones 2000-2017

Total Dow Jones Industrial Average Return – 117.576%

Annualized Dow Jones Industrial Average Return – 4.434%

---

[6] Data - www.dqydj.com/dow-jones-return-calculator/

Total DJIA Return (Dividends Reinvested) – 234.254%

Annualized DJIA Return (Dividends Reinvested) – 6.967%

- **New Highs**: 6 significant highs.
    - The Dow reached **11,722** in **March 2000** and crossed **16,000** in **2013**.
- **New Lows**: 2 significant lows.
    - The Dow dropped after the **9/11 attacks** in 2001, falling to **8,920.70**.
    - Another low occurred during the **2008 financial crisis**, with the Dow hitting **6,547.05** in **March 2009**.

Major Events:

- **Dot Com Bubble Burst:** 2000-2002 - NASDAQ fell from 5,048 to 1,139.
- **2000 Presidential Election**: November 7, 2000 – George W. Bush was elected President after a contentious recount in Florida.
- **Enron and Author Andersen Financial Scandal**: 2001- Energy company of 85,000 employees found to be using fraudulent accounting practices

- **9/11 Terrorist Attacks**: September 11, 2001 – Al-Qaeda terrorists attack the World Trade Center and the Pentagon.
- **War in Afghanistan**: October 7, 2001 – August 30, 2021.
- **Iraq War**: March 20, 2003 – December 18, 2011 – U.S. invades Iraq to topple Saddam Hussein.
- **Global Financial Crisis**: 2007-2008 – U.S. housing bubble bursts, leading to severe economic recession.
- **2008 Presidential Election**: November 4, 2008 – Barack Obama was elected the first African American President.
- **Death of Osama bin Laden**: May 2, 2011 – U.S. Navy SEALs kill the mastermind behind 9/11.
- **2012 Presidential Election**: November 6, 2012 – Barack Obama re-elected as President.
- **Boston Marathon Terrorist Attacks**: April 15, 2013.
- **2016 Presidential Election**: November 8, 2016 – Donald Trump was elected President.

Recession and the Markets:

Early 2000s Recession (Dot-Com Bubble)

- **Duration**: March 2001 – November 2001 (8 months)
- **Stock Market Impact**:
    o The DJIA fell by around 27% from early 2000 to late 2002 as the dot-com bubble burst and corporate accounting scandals (e.g., Enron) emerged.
    o The 9/11 terrorist attacks exacerbated the market downturn in 2001.

Great Recession (2007-2009)

- **Duration**: December 2007 – June 2009 (18 months)
- **Stock Market Impact**:
    o The DJIA lost about 54% of its value from October 2007 to March 2009, as the subprime mortgage crisis and the collapse of Lehman Brothers led to a global financial crisis.

- The market began a prolonged recovery in March 2009, eventually leading to the longest bull market in U.S. history.

The beginning of the 21st century brought unprecedented challenges and opportunities for the U.S. economy and stock market. The optimism of the late 1990s, fueled by the tech boom, quickly turned to anxiety as the dot-com bubble burst in 2000, wiping out billions in market value and leading to a sharp economic downturn. In 2001, the U.S. faced another major blow with the tragic events of September 11, 2001 (9/11), which sent shockwaves through the economy and stock market.

Despite these setbacks, the U.S. economy showed resilience, bouncing back in the mid-2000s before being hit again by the 2008 financial crisis. This chapter will examine the dot-com bust, the economic impact of 9/11, the 2008 financial crisis, and the recovery that followed leading up to 2017.

7.1 The Bursting of the Dot-Com Bubble

The dot-com bubble was a speculative frenzy that gripped the U.S. stock market during the late 1990s, particularly in the technology sector. Fueled by the rapid rise of the internet and the potential for new online business models, investors poured money into tech startups, many of which had little or no earnings. By 2000, the stock prices of internet-based companies had reached astronomical levels, with the NASDAQ Composite Index rising more than 500% between 1995 and early 2000. However, as it became clear that many of these companies were overvalued and lacked sustainable business models, the bubble burst, leading to a sharp market decline.

7.1.1 The Rise of the Dot-Com Era

In the late 1990s, the advent of the internet created a sense of boundless optimism about the future of technology and its potential to reshape the global economy. Startups with little more than a business plan and a website were able to raise millions of dollars from venture capitalists and investors eager to capitalize on the new digital frontier. Companies like

Amazon, Yahoo!, and eBay quickly became household names, and their stock prices soared as investors believed these firms would dominate the new online economy.

Initial public offerings (IPOs) became the norm for tech startups, with many companies going public before they had even turned a profit. The frenzy around these IPOs was driven by speculative fervor, as investors bet that the internet would lead to an economic revolution. In many cases, traditional metrics for valuing companies, such as earnings and revenue, were ignored in favor of vague promises of future growth. The dot-com boom was fueled by a belief that "eyeballs"—the number of people visiting a website—were more important than profits.

7.1.2 The Crash of 2000-2002

By early 2000, cracks in the dot-com bubble began to appear. Investors started to question the sustainability of the sky-high valuations of many tech companies, especially those that had yet to turn a profit. As these concerns grew, the NASDAQ peaked in March 2000 at over 5,000 points before beginning a sharp and prolonged decline.

The bursting of the dot-com bubble had devastating effects on the stock market and the broader economy. By October 2002, the NASDAQ had lost over 75% of its value, and many tech companies went bankrupt. The IPO market dried up, venture capital funding shrank, and investors who had bet heavily on tech stocks saw their portfolios wiped out. Major firms like Pets.com and Webvan became symbols of the era's excesses, collapsing after burning through millions in investor capital.

The broader stock market was also affected by the collapse of the tech sector. The S&P 500, which the rise of tech stocks had buoyed, experienced a significant downturn, with the index losing more than 40% of its value between 2000 and 2002. Corporate scandals, such as those involving Enron and WorldCom, further eroded investor confidence, as accounting fraud and mismanagement were revealed at some of the largest corporations in the country.

7.1.3 Economic Consequences of the Dot-Com Bust

The dot-com bubble's collapse led to a sharp economic downturn in the early 2000s, often referred to as the "dot-com recession." Unemployment rose as tech companies laid off workers, and investment in the technology sector dried up. The Federal Reserve, under Chairman Alan Greenspan, responded by cutting interest rates to stimulate economic activity and prevent a deeper recession.

The broader economy did eventually recover from the dot-com bust, but the collapse left deep scars on investor confidence. The speculative excesses of the late 1990s, where companies with little revenue or profit potential were given sky-high valuations, forced a significant reevaluation of market behavior. Investors, who had been overly enthusiastic about the promise of tech startups, became far more cautious in the years following the crash. This newfound caution contributed to a shift in market focus toward companies with strong fundamentals, solid earnings, and more traditional business models. Additionally, the collapse exposed how overly speculative investing can lead to unsustainable bubbles, making investors more wary of irrational exuberance in the future. This shift may have contributed to the rotation from stock market investments to real estate, eventually playing a role in the formation of the 2007 housing bubble.

The aftermath of the dot-com crash also led to increased scrutiny of corporate governance and financial reporting practices. High-profile accounting scandals at companies like Enron and WorldCom during the early 2000s further undermined public trust in corporate management and highlighted the need for greater transparency. In response, Congress passed the Sarbanes-Oxley Act in 2002, which introduced stricter regulations on financial disclosures and corporate accountability. The act mandated that top executives take personal responsibility for the accuracy of financial reports, imposed more rigorous auditing standards, and increased penalties for corporate fraud. These reforms aimed to restore investor confidence and prevent the types of abuses that contributed to the dot-com bubble and subsequent financial collapses, reshaping the regulatory landscape of the U.S. stock market for years to come.

7.2 The Effects of the 9/11 Terrorist Attacks on the Market

The U.S. stock market faced an unprecedented crisis in 2001 with the devastating terrorist attacks on September 11, 2001 (9/11). The attacks, targeting the World Trade Center in New York City and the Pentagon in Washington, D.C., claimed thousands of innocent lives, leaving a nation heartbroken. But the impact went beyond the immeasurable human tragedy—shockwaves rippled through the U.S. economy and financial markets, adding a sense of collective grief and fear to an already fragile landscape.

7.2.1 The Immediate Economic Impact of 9/11

In the immediate aftermath of 9/11, the country was paralyzed by fear and uncertainty. New York City's financial district, a global economic hub, was in chaos. The New York Stock Exchange (NYSE) and NASDAQ were forced to close, marking the longest shutdown of U.S. financial markets since the Great Depression.

When the markets reopened on September 17, 2001, a deep sense of loss hung over Wall Street. The Dow Jones Industrial Average (DJIA) plummeted by over 600 points, nearly 7%, the largest single-day point loss in history at that time. The emotional toll on investors and traders, many of whom had lost colleagues or loved ones, was palpable as they returned to work amid the ashes of the World Trade Center.

The economic fallout was especially brutal for specific industries. Airlines, travel, and hospitality were devastated as air travel was temporarily grounded and the public's confidence in flying collapsed. The stock prices of major airlines like American Airlines and United Airlines tumbled, and many carriers were pushed to the brink of bankruptcy in the years that followed. The destruction of the World Trade Center, home to numerous financial institutions, caused widespread business disruption and laid bare the vulnerability of the global economy.

Thousands of businesses were affected, and layoffs surged as companies scrambled to cut costs. The psychological impact of the attacks lingered, fueling a slowdown in economic activity. Fear of future attacks loomed over consumers and investors alike, deepening the uncertainty and adding to the economic wounds that would take years to heal.

7.2.2 Government Response and Economic Recovery

In response to the 9/11 attacks, the U.S. government implemented a series of policies aimed at stabilizing the economy and restoring public confidence. The Federal

Reserve, under Chairman Alan Greenspan, moved quickly to lower interest rates, cutting the federal funds rate from 3.5% to 1.75% by the end of 2001. This aggressive monetary easing was intended to boost economic activity by making borrowing cheaper for businesses and consumers.

The U.S. government also passed a series of stimulus measures to support the economy. The Airline Stabilization Act provided $15 billion in financial aid to the struggling airline industry, while the Economic Stimulus Act of 2002 included tax cuts and increased government spending to spur growth.

Despite the initial economic shock caused by 9/11, the U.S. economy showed resilience. By 2003, the economy was growing again, and the stock market began to recover. The DJIA, which had fallen sharply after the attacks, rebounded by 2004 as investor confidence returned and businesses adapted to the post-9/11 security environment.

7.2.3 The Impact of 9/11 on Global Markets

The effects of 9/11 were not confined to U.S. soil; the shockwaves spread rapidly across the globe, impacting international markets in profound ways. In the immediate aftermath, stock markets around the world plunged as investors feared the onset of a broader geopolitical crisis. Major indices, such as the FTSE 100 in London, DAX in Germany, and the Nikkei 225 in Japan, saw sharp declines, mirroring the losses on Wall Street. The sheer scale and symbolism of the attacks on the U.S., the world's largest economy and a major player in global finance, created widespread panic. Investors pulled out of risky assets, driving a flight to safety as they poured money into gold, bonds, and other traditionally safer investments. The interconnectivity of the global economy became more evident than ever, as disruptions in the U.S. financial system rippled across international markets, disrupting global trade, investment flows, and consumer confidence worldwide.

Beyond the immediate financial fallout, 9/11 led to a fundamental reevaluation of global security risks. The attacks demonstrated that terrorism could have far-reaching economic consequences, forcing investors and corporations to consider the potential for geopolitical events to upend financial markets and disrupt business operations. This growing awareness of "terrorism risk" became a central factor in investment strategies and risk management, particularly for multinational corporations. The insurance industry faced unprecedented challenges as the scale of claims related to property damage, business interruption, and life insurance soared. Insurers were forced to pay out billions in claims, leading to a significant restructuring of the industry. In response, the concept of terrorism insurance emerged, and governments around the world, including the U.S., introduced legislation to backstop the insurance industry against catastrophic losses from future attacks. This new layer of financial risk management reflected the long-lasting impact of 9/11, as the world adapted to a new reality where global markets were increasingly vulnerable to geopolitical and security threats.

7.3 The Housing Bubble and Financial Crisis of 2008

While the U.S. economy recovered from the dot-com bust and the impact of 9/11, the seeds of the next major financial crisis were being sown in the housing market. The mid-2000s saw a dramatic rise in home prices, driven by easy access to credit, low interest rates, and speculative investment in real estate. However, by 2007, it became clear that the housing market was in a bubble, and when it burst, it triggered the most severe financial crisis since the Great Depression.

7.3.1 The Rise of the Housing Bubble

The housing bubble was fueled by factors, including low interest rates, lax lending standards, and the widespread belief that home prices would continue to rise indefinitely. In the years following the dot-com bust, the Federal Reserve kept interest rates low to stimulate economic growth. This made borrowing cheaper for homebuyers, leading to a surge in demand for housing.

At the same time, mortgage lenders began offering subprime loans to borrowers with poor credit histories. These loans were often structured with low introductory interest rates that would reset to higher levels after a few years, making them affordable in the short term but potentially unsustainable in the long term. Many borrowers took on mortgages they could not afford, betting that rising home prices would allow them to refinance or sell their homes at a profit.

The rise of mortgage-backed securities (MBS) and collateralized debt obligations (CDOs) played a pivotal role in inflating the housing bubble. These financial instruments fundamentally changed the way mortgages were financed, creating an entirely new market for investment. Banks and financial institutions bundled home loans into securities—MBS—that could be sold to a wide range of investors, including pension funds, hedge funds, and international financial institutions. The underlying idea was that by pooling numerous mortgages together, the risk of individual defaults would be spread across the bundle, making these securities appear relatively safe, even for risky borrowers. CDOs took this innovation further by bundling MBS and other types of debt into more complex products, which divided the risk into different tranches for investors with varying risk appetites. The introduction of MBS and CDOs led to significant profits for Wall Street firms and a surge in demand for mortgage loans, fueling a financial frenzy that drove the housing market to new heights.

However, as the demand for MBS and CDOs grew, banks and lenders began issuing increasingly risky mortgages to meet the supply needed for these investments. The housing market became speculative, and the quality of the underlying mortgages started to deteriorate. Subprime mortgages, given to borrowers with poor credit histories, became widespread as lending standards loosened dramatically. Despite the high-risk nature of these loans, they were bundled into MBS and CDOs, with many of these securities still being rated as low-risk by rating agencies.

As home prices continued to rise, the true danger of these financial products was obscured, but when the housing market cooled and prices fell, large numbers of borrowers defaulted on their loans. This triggered a collapse in the value of MBS and CDOs, spreading losses across global financial markets and ultimately leading to financial crisis. The unchecked growth of these complex financial products, coupled with a failure to recognize or address the deteriorating quality of loans, turned the housing bubble into a global economic catastrophe.

7.3.2 The Financial Crisis of 2008

By 2007, cracks in the housing market began to appear. Home prices in many parts of the country had reached unsustainable levels. As interest rates on adjustable-rate mortgages began to reset, many borrowers could not make their payments. Foreclosures surged, and the value of mortgage-backed securities plummeted, leading to massive losses for banks and investors.

The housing market's collapse triggered a broader financial crisis, as major financial institutions faced insolvency. In September 2008, Lehman Brothers, one of the largest investment banks in the world, filed for bankruptcy, setting off a chain reaction of panic in global financial markets. The stock market experienced a sharp decline, with the S&P 500 losing more than 50% of its value between 2007 and bottoming out March 9, 2009.

The financial crisis had far-reaching consequences for the global economy. Unemployment soared as businesses cut back on spending and investment, and consumer confidence plummeted. The banking system, which had been at the center of the crisis, was brought to the brink of collapse, with several major banks requiring government bailouts to survive.

7.3.3 Government Response to the Crisis

In response to the financial crisis, the U.S. government and the Federal Reserve implemented unprecedented measures to stabilize the economy. The Federal Reserve, under Chairman

Ben Bernanke, slashed interest rates to near zero and implemented a policy of quantitative easing (QE), in which the central bank purchased large quantities of government bonds and mortgage-backed securities to inject liquidity into the financial system.

The U.S. government took extraordinary steps to stabilize the economy and prevent the collapse of key financial institutions. One of the most significant measures was the Emergency Economic Stabilization Act (EESA), passed in October 2008. This legislation created the Troubled Asset Relief Program (TARP), which allocated $700 billion in bailout funds to banks, insurance companies, and other financial institutions that were on the brink of collapse. The primary goal of TARP was to restore liquidity to the banking system, which had been severely disrupted by the rapid devaluation of mortgage-backed securities and other toxic assets. By purchasing these troubled assets and providing capital to struggling institutions, the government aimed to prevent a complete breakdown of the financial system, which would have had devastating effects on the broader economy.

One of the key recipients of TARP funds was American International Group (AIG), a global insurance giant that had been deeply involved in insuring mortgage-backed securities and other complex financial products. As the housing market collapsed and defaults skyrocketed, AIG found itself unable to cover the massive claims it faced on its credit default swaps—essentially insurance policies on these failing securities.

Without government intervention, AIG's failure would have caused a ripple effect throughout the global financial system, as many large banks and institutions were heavily exposed to AIG's obligations. To prevent this systemic risk, the U.S. government stepped in with a $182 billion bailout for AIG, providing the liquidity necessary to meet its obligations and stabilizing the markets. This bailout was critical in preventing a cascade of additional failures, as AIG was so interconnected with other major institutions that its collapse could have triggered a broader economic meltdown. The U.S. government's intervention, through both TARP and the AIG bailout, was designed to shore up confidence in the financial system and prevent the crisis from worsening.

Despite the initial panic, the government's actions helped stabilize the financial system, and by 2009, the economy began to show signs of recovery. The stock market, which had hit a low in March 2009, started to rebound as investors regained confidence in the economic outlook.

7.4 The Recovery and Economic Expansion (2009-2017)

The recovery from the 2008 financial crisis was slow but steady, with the U.S. economy gradually returning to growth in the years following the crisis. The stock market, buoyed by low interest rates and government stimulus, entered a new bull market, with the S&P 500 doubling in value between 2009 and 2013. However, the recovery was uneven, with many Americans still struggling with the effects of unemployment, wage stagnation, and rising inequality.

7.4.1 The Stock Market's Bull Run

The stock market's recovery from the 2008 financial crisis was remarkable. By 2013, the S&P 500 had surpassed its pre-crisis peak, and by 2017, it had nearly tripled in value from its 2009 low. The bull market was driven by a combination of factors, including low interest rates, corporate earnings growth, and the

Federal Reserve's continued economic support through quantitative easing.

Technology stocks, in particular, played a key role in driving the market's growth. Companies like Apple, Amazon, Google (now Alphabet), and Facebook became some of the most valuable companies in the world as the rise of smartphones, e-commerce, and social media transformed the global economy. Investors flocked to these tech giants, which were seen as the leaders of the new digital economy.

7.4.2 Challenges and Inequality in the Recovery

While the stock market experienced a strong recovery, the broader economy faced significant challenges. Unemployment, which had peaked at 10% in 2009, gradually fell, but many workers who had lost their jobs during the recession struggled to find new employment. Wage growth remained sluggish, and the economic recovery was marked by rising income inequality, as the benefits of the stock market's gains were concentrated among wealthier Americans.

The housing market also took years to recover, with many homeowners who had lost their homes during the crisis unable to reenter the market. The rise of "underwater" mortgages, in which homeowners owed more on their homes than they were worth, further dampened the recovery in the housing sector.

Despite these challenges, the U.S. economy continued to grow throughout the 2010s, with GDP expanding steadily. By 2017, the U.S. was experiencing one of the longest economic expansions in its history, and the stock market was reaching new all-time highs.

Chapter 8
The New Millennium (2018-Today)

Bull Market – Expansion

Dow Jones Industrial

January 1, 2018 – 24719.22

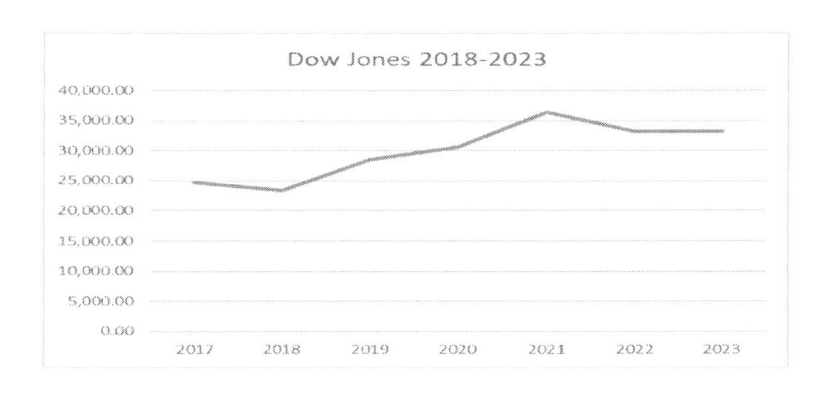

Dow Jones 2018-2023

Total Dow Jones Industrial Average Return – 43.187%

Annualized Dow Jones Industrial Average Return – 6.255%

Total DJIA Return (Dividends Reinvested) – 61.450%

Annualized DJIA Return (Dividends Reinvested) – 8.433%

- **New Highs**: 7 significant highs.
    - The Dow hit **29,000** in **January 2020** and later reached **36,000** in early **2023**.
- **New Lows**: 1 significant low.
    - The Dow fell to **18,591.93** in **March 2020** due to the COVID-19 pandemic.

Major Events:

- **2020 Presidential Election**: November 3, 2020 – Joe Biden was elected president.
- **COVID-19 Pandemic**: March 2020 onwards – Global pandemic caused economic and health crises.
- **Pandemic Market Crash**: March 16, 2020 – Dow Jones fell 12.93% or 2997.10 points.
- **Capitol Riot**: January 6, 2021 – Supporters of Donald Trump stormed the U.S. Capitol.
- **U.S. Withdrawal from Afghanistan**: August 30, 2021 – Ended the 20-year war.
- **U.S. Inflation:** 2022 - In 2022, the US inflation rate reached 9.1% in the middle of the year, which was one

of the highest rates since 1981. This forced the Federal Reserve to increase the fed rate 11 times between March 2022 and July 2023.

Recession and the Markets:

COVID-19 Recession

- **Duration**: February 2020 – April 2020 (2 months)
- **Stock Market Impact**:
    o The Dow dropped more than 35% from February to March 2020 due to global lockdowns and economic shutdowns caused by the COVID-19 pandemic.
    o A swift recovery followed as fiscal stimulus and Federal Reserve interventions stabilized markets, with the Dow reaching new highs by the end of 2020.

The years from 2018 to the present have been marked by significant economic shifts, political changes, and technological advancements that continue to reshape the global financial landscape. The period began with a robust U.S.

economy, characterized by strong stock market performance and historically low unemployment rates.

However, the advent of the COVID-19 pandemic in 2020 upended this progress, plunging the global economy into a sharp recession. The subsequent recovery has been uneven, with supply chain disruptions, inflationary pressures, and political unrest affecting markets worldwide. This chapter will examine the economic trends of the late 2010s, the profound impact of the COVID-19 pandemic on the stock market and global economy, and the recovery and new challenges that have emerged as the world adjusts to a post-pandemic reality.

8.1 Economic Trends Leading Up to 2020

The U.S. economy entered 2018 with strong momentum. The recovery from the 2008 financial crisis had produced one of the longest economic expansions in U.S. history. By the late 2010s, key economic indicators such as unemployment, GDP growth, and stock market performance were reaching impressive levels. However, there were signs of potential vulnerability beneath the surface, particularly in rising corporate debt and political uncertainty.

8.1.1 Stock Market Growth and Corporate Tax Cuts

One of the most significant factors driving the stock market's strong performance was the Tax Cuts and Jobs Act (TCJA), signed into law by President Donald Trump in December 2017. The TCJA lowered the corporate tax rate from 35% to 21%, leading to a surge in corporate profits and stock buybacks. Companies used the windfall from the tax cuts to return capital to shareholders, driving up stock prices and further fueling the bull market that had begun in 2009.

The tax cuts were particularly beneficial for large corporations, many of which reported record profits in 2018 and 2019. Technology companies, such as Apple, Amazon, and Alphabet (Google's parent company), continued to lead the stock market's growth as their dominance in sectors like e-commerce, cloud computing, and digital advertising solidified. The S&P 500, which had experienced a strong run throughout the 2010s, reached new all-time highs in 2018 and 2019.

While the stock market experienced significant gains, concerns about income inequality and corporate debt began to emerge. Critics argued that the benefits of the Tax Cuts and Jobs Act

(TCJA) were disproportionately skewed toward wealthy individuals and large corporations, with minimal trickle-down effect on middle- and lower-income Americans. Many felt that the anticipated widespread economic benefits had not materialized for the broader population, particularly for those outside of the upper income brackets.

Additionally, the increase in stock buybacks raised questions about corporate financial health, as many companies were taking on debt to fund these buybacks. This raised concerns about the potential vulnerabilities on corporate balance sheets, with some critics pointing out that this approach could leave businesses more exposed to economic downturns. While boosting stock prices in the short term, the reliance on borrowing for buybacks heightened the risk that companies could face financial challenges if economic conditions deteriorated.

8.1.2 Record-Low Unemployment and Wage Stagnation

By 2019, the U.S. unemployment rate had fallen to its lowest level in decades, reaching 3.5%. The strong labor market was one of the economy's bright spots as job creation continued to outpace expectations. However, despite the low unemployment rate, wage growth remained relatively stagnant. Many workers, particularly those in lower-wage industries, saw only modest increases in their earnings, and income inequality remained a persistent issue.

The rise of the gig economy and the increasing prevalence of part-time and contract work also contributed to wage stagnation. While the gig economy provided flexibility for workers, it often lacked the benefits and stability of traditional full-time employment. This created a divide between workers in high-paying industries, such as technology and finance, and those in lower-wage sectors, where wages struggled to keep pace with the rising cost of living.

8.2 The Impact of the COVID-19 Pandemic on the Market

The outbreak of the COVID-19 pandemic in early 2020 marked one of the most significant economic disruptions in modern history. As governments worldwide implemented lockdowns and social distancing measures to contain the spread of the virus, the global economy ground to a halt. The stock market, which had reached new highs as recently as

February 2020, experienced one of the most severe sell-offs since the 2008 financial crisis. However, the subsequent recovery, driven by unprecedented government intervention and monetary stimulus, has been remarkable and uneven.

8.2.1 The Stock Market's Initial Crash

In March 2020, as the scale of the pandemic became clear, global financial markets entered a state of panic. The U.S. stock market experienced dramatic declines, with the S&P 500 losing nearly 34% of its value in just a few weeks. The speed and severity of the market crash were unprecedented as investors scrambled to assess the economic fallout from the pandemic.

The sudden shutdown of entire sectors of the economy, including travel, hospitality, and retail, led to a sharp increase in unemployment, with millions of workers losing their jobs or being furloughed. The U.S. unemployment rate surged to 14.8% in April 2020, the highest level since the Great Depression. Consumer spending plummeted, businesses faced unprecedented challenges as supply chains were disrupted, and demand evaporated.

The uncertainty surrounding the virus exacerbated the panic in financial markets. With no clear timeline for when the pandemic would be brought under control, investors were unsure of how long the economic downturn would last. Volatility in the stock market reached extreme levels, with the CBOE Volatility Index (VIX), often referred to as the "fear index," spiking to its highest point since the 2008 financial crisis.

8.2.2 Government Intervention and Stimulus Measures

In response to the economic crisis, governments around the world implemented a series of unprecedented stimulus measures. In the U.S., the Federal Reserve took immediate action to stabilize financial markets, cutting interest rates to near zero and launching massive asset purchase programs, known as quantitative easing (QE). The Fed's intervention helped restore liquidity to the financial system and reassured investors that the central bank was committed to supporting the economy.

At the same time, the U.S. government passed the Coronavirus Aid, Relief, and Economic Security (CARES) Act in March

2020, a $2.2 trillion stimulus package designed to provide direct financial support to individuals, businesses, and healthcare providers. The CARES Act included provisions for enhanced unemployment benefits, direct stimulus payments to Americans, and loans and grants to small businesses through the Paycheck Protection Program (PPP). These measures helped mitigate the economic damage caused by the pandemic and provided a lifeline to millions of Americans who had lost their jobs or seen their incomes reduced.

While the government's swift response prevented a deeper recession, it also had significant long-term implications. The massive increase in government spending and the expansion of the Federal Reserve's balance sheet raised concerns about inflation and the sustainability of government debt. In addition, the stock market's rapid recovery, fueled by low interest rates and monetary stimulus, led to concerns about asset bubbles and income inequality.

8.2.3 The Stock Market's Rapid Recovery

Despite the severity of the initial market crash, the U.S. stock market rebounded remarkably quickly. By August 2020, the

S&P 500 had regained all of its pandemic-related losses, and by the end of the year, it had reached new all-time highs. The stock market's rapid recovery was driven by a combination of factors, including the Federal Reserve's aggressive monetary policy, government stimulus measures, and investor optimism about the development of COVID-19 vaccines.

The technology sector played a critical role in the market's recovery. As lockdowns and social distancing measures forced people to work, shop, and socialize online, technology companies saw a surge in demand for their products and services. Companies like Amazon, Apple, and Microsoft reported record earnings in 2020 as consumers shifted to e-commerce, remote work, and digital entertainment. The NASDAQ Composite Index, heavily weighted toward technology stocks, outperformed the broader market, reaching new highs by the summer of 2020.

While the stock market's recovery was swift, the broader economy remained in a state of uncertainty. Many sectors, particularly those reliant on in-person interactions, such as hospitality and retail, continued to struggle. Small businesses faced significant challenges, with many forced to close permanently. The recovery was uneven, with high-income earners and large corporations benefiting from rising asset prices, while lower-income workers and small businesses bore the brunt of the economic fallout.

8.3 Economic Recovery and the Challenges of 2021-2022

As vaccines were developed and distributed in late 2020 and early 2021, there was a renewed sense of hope for a return to normal life. After months of uncertainty and loss, the U.S. economy began to show signs of recovery. Businesses reopened, people returned to work, and unemployment began to fall. However, the path to recovery was not without its challenges. The scars left by the pandemic—both in human lives lost and the economic toll—remained, and new issues surfaced, including supply chain disruptions, labor shortages, and rising inflation. These factors made the road to economic stability more complex than anticipated.

8.3.1 Supply Chain Disruptions and Labor Shortages

One of the most significant hurdles to the global economy in 2021 was the disruption of supply chains. The pandemic had caused factory shutdowns and interruptions in transportation networks, creating a bottleneck in the production and distribution of goods. As demand for products surged in 2021, supply chains struggled to keep up, leading to widespread shortages. From semiconductors to everyday consumer goods, businesses found it increasingly difficult to meet customer demand, causing frustration for both companies and consumers alike. These disruptions rippled through the economy, contributing to rising prices for goods and services and leaving industries like automotive manufacturing particularly hard-hit, as a shortage of semiconductors led to delays in production and higher prices for new and used cars.

At the same time, labor shortages added another layer of complexity to the recovery. Many workers who had been displaced during the pandemic were slow to return to the workforce, often citing health and safety concerns, difficulties with childcare, or the availability of enhanced unemployment benefits. Sectors like hospitality, manufacturing, and retail struggled to fill positions, forcing businesses to raise wages and cope with increased operating costs. For many companies, this meant higher prices for consumers, adding to the broader economic strain. This combination of disrupted supply chains and labor shortages left a lasting impact on daily life, with many still feeling the effects long after businesses had reopened.

8.3.2 Rising Inflation and Federal Reserve Policy

As the U.S. economy rebounded from the pandemic, inflation emerged as a significant concern. By mid-2021, inflation had reached its highest level in decades, with the Consumer Price Index (CPI) rising 5.4% year-over-year in July 2021, the largest increase since 2008. This spike was driven by a combination of supply chain disruptions, labor shortages, and a surge in consumer demand as the economy reopened. The cost of everyday essentials, such as gasoline, which increased by 45% between June 2020 and June 2021, and groceries, which saw a 4.5% rise during the same period, put significant pressure on household budgets. These rising costs sparked concerns about the long-term sustainability of the economic recovery, particularly as wage growth in many sectors lagged behind inflation.

The Federal Reserve, which had kept interest rates near zero since the start of the pandemic to stimulate the economy, faced a complex challenge in managing these inflationary pressures.

Initially, the Fed characterized the inflation spike as "transitory," attributing it to temporary factors like supply chain bottlenecks that would ease over time. However, by late 2021, with the CPI still elevated—hitting 6.8% in November 2021, the highest in nearly 40 years—it became clear that inflation was more persistent than anticipated. In response, the Fed signaled its intention to tighten monetary policy in 2022, including reducing its asset purchases (which had reached $120 billion per month in 2020) and gradually raising interest rates. While these actions were viewed as necessary to curb inflation, they also raised concerns about potential market volatility and slower economic growth, particularly in interest rate-sensitive sectors like housing.

The prospect of higher interest rates had significant implications for the stock market and the broader economy. Low interest rates had been a key driver of the stock market's rapid recovery during the pandemic. As the Fed shifted towards tighter monetary policy, concerns about the potential for market corrections grew, particularly in sectors that had benefited from the low-interest-rate environment. Investors also worried about the impact of higher borrowing costs on businesses and consumers, which could slow down the economic recovery. Balancing inflation control with economic growth became a central focus for policymakers, businesses, and consumers alike as they navigated the uncertainties of a post-pandemic economy.

8.4 The Future of the Stock Market and Global Economy

The global economy is still grappling with the aftermath of the COVID-19 pandemic and the challenges of the post-pandemic recovery. The 2022 stock market was volatile, with the Federal Reserve raising rates 11 times for a total hike of 5.25% between March 2022 and July 2023. We also witnessed international tensions which saw the Dow slip 8.78% for the year. However, 2023 was markedly better and more stable with a return of 13.7%. Labor, technology, inflation and globalization, continue to play a central role in determining the future of the financial markets.

8.4.1 Technological Innovation and the New Economy

One of the defining features of the post-pandemic world is the acceleration of technological innovation. The pandemic forced businesses and consumers to adopt new technologies faster than ever before, leading to lasting changes in how people work, shop, and interact. The rise of remote work, for example, has led to a shift in demand for office space and reshaped the real estate market. At the same time, the growth of e-commerce has further solidified the dominance of technology companies in the global economy.

Looking ahead, technological innovation is likely to continue driving economic growth and transforming industries. Advances in artificial intelligence, automation, and renewable energy are expected to create new opportunities for investors and businesses while posing challenges for workers and policymakers.

8.4.2 Geopolitical Tensions and Global Trade

Another key factor shaping the stock market's and global economy's future is the ongoing geopolitical tensions between major powers, particularly the U.S. and China. The trade war between the two countries, which began under the Trump administration, has raised concerns about the future of globalization and the stability of global supply chains. The relationship between the U.S. and China will continue to be a major factor in global economic trends as both countries compete for dominance in areas such as technology, trade, and military power. Additionally, other geopolitical risks, including tensions in the Middle East, the rise of populist movements in Europe, and the ongoing challenges of climate change, will have significant implications for the global economy and financial markets.

The conflict between Russia and Ukraine, which began in 2022, has also had a profound impact on global markets. The war has disrupted supply chains, particularly in energy and agriculture, leading to increased volatility in commodity prices. The ongoing conflict has strained relations between Russia and Western countries, resulting in economic sanctions that have further complicated global trade dynamics.

In the Middle East, the conflict between Israel and Hamas has escalated, adding another layer of uncertainty to the region. This conflict has the potential to affect global oil prices and investor sentiment, particularly if it leads to broader regional instability.

These geopolitical tensions, combined with the existing challenges of inflation and rising interest rates, create a complex environment for investors. As the world navigates these uncertainties, the interplay between geopolitical events and economic policies will continue to shape the future of the stock market and global economy.

8.4.3 The Long-Term Outlook

The long-term outlook for the stock market and global economy remains uncertain as the world adjusts to the changes brought about by the COVID-19 pandemic. While the stock market has rebounded in the face of unprecedented challenges, the risks of inflation, rising interest rates, and geopolitical instability could lead to increased volatility in the years ahead.

However, despite these challenges, the U.S. economy has shown a remarkable ability to adapt and innovate in the face of adversity. The rise of new technologies, the labor market's resilience, and the U.S. consumer's ongoing strength suggest that the economy is well-positioned to weather future storms. As we move further into the new millennium, the lessons of the past will continue to inform the decisions of investors, policymakers, and businesses as they navigate the ever-changing landscape of the global economy.

Conclusion
Learning from the Generational Cycles

Introduction to the Cycles: Lessons from History

Throughout the history of the U.S. stock market, the generational cycles have revealed important lessons about resilience, innovation, and recovery. Each cycle—whether characterized by expansion, contraction, or a mix of the two—has reflected the underlying economic and social forces of the time. The expansion cycles have consistently brought periods of prosperity, technological innovation, and financial growth, while the contraction cycles have tested the resolve of investors and businesses alike. But what is remarkable is that, over time, each contraction has laid the groundwork for an even stronger expansion. As demonstrated throughout this book, the stock market's long-term trajectory, despite its periods of volatility, continues to rise. Always to be stated, that does not mean markets are guaranteed to rise and past performance does not guarantee future results. But also as has been previously stated, history doesn't always repeat, but it does often rhyme.

These cycles aren't just about financial returns; they are reflections of broader societal patterns. The roaring 1920s, for instance, saw unprecedented economic growth as America embraced industrialization and urbanization. However, the exuberance of this period was followed by the Great Depression, a stark reminder of the dangers of over-leverage and speculation. Similarly, the post-World War II boom brought unparalleled prosperity, only to be tempered by the stagflation of the 1970s. Yet, the lessons learned during these contraction periods paved the way for innovations that fueled future growth. Each recovery was stronger than the last, showing that while downturns are inevitable, they are also part of a larger cycle of regeneration.

The Significance of the Cycles: Navigating Expansion and Contraction

By examining the historical returns of these generational cycles, we can see a pattern of growing resilience and adaptability. In every cycle, whether expansionary or contractionary, the stock market has ultimately emerged stronger, delivering higher long-term returns. Investors who took a long-term perspective and understood the cyclical nature of markets were often rewarded with impressive gains.

Consider the 1982-1999 expansionary cycle. During this period, the stock market experienced robust growth driven by advancements in technology, deregulation, and a boom in consumer confidence. The Dow Jones grew by an astounding 1218.626% from 1982 to 1999, reflecting the growth in global trade, the rise of the internet, and the increasing efficiency of capital markets. The lessons from this era were clear: technological innovation and financial deregulation could unlock incredible economic potential.

However, no expansion lasts indefinitely, and the dot-com bubble of the early 2000s served as a reminder of the dangers of speculative excess. When the bubble burst, the market entered another contraction, but once again, it was a contraction that set the stage for future growth. The post-dot-com recovery, coupled with advancements in digital technology, ultimately helped the markets shake off an amazing amount of turmoil. During this generational contraction period from 2000-2017, the Dow Jones was able to average a yearly return of 4.34% and 6.69% if dividends were reinvested.

The cyclical nature of the market is not a pattern to be feared, but rather one to be understood and embraced. Each contraction has taught investors critical lessons about risk management, the importance of diversification, and the dangers of speculative excess. In contrast, each expansion has reminded us of the market's capacity for growth, innovation, and wealth creation when conditions are right.

Technological Innovation: AI and the Future of Productivity

Looking ahead, one of the most promising forces driving the next expansion cycle is artificial intelligence (AI). Just as the industrial revolution, electrification, and the rise of the internet transformed the global economy in previous cycles, AI is poised to reshape entire industries. From automation and machine learning to natural language processing and robotics, AI is making businesses more efficient and unlocking new levels of productivity.

The impact of AI on the economy is already being felt in a variety of sectors. In manufacturing, AI-powered machines are streamlining production processes, reducing waste, and improving quality control. In finance, AI algorithms are being used to optimize investment strategies, detect fraud, and improve customer service through advanced data analysis. In healthcare, AI is enabling faster and more accurate diagnostics, personalizing treatment plans, and accelerating drug discovery. The potential applications of AI are vast, and its ability to increase productivity and drive innovation will likely have far-reaching implications for economic growth and stock market returns in the coming decades.

In previous cycles, technological advancements such as railroads during the 19th century or the internet in the late 20th century were critical drivers of expansion. The stock market has always been a reflection of society's ability to innovate, and AI represents the next frontier in that innovation. McKinsey Global Institute estimates that AI could add $13 trillion to the global economy by 2030, an indication of the profound effect this technology will have on growth.

Much like the dot-com boom, the AI revolution will undoubtedly bring periods of speculation, overvaluation, and correction. But as with all generational cycles, the long-term impact of AI is likely to be transformative, leading to new business models, increased productivity, and greater economic expansion. AI-driven efficiency and automation could very well help address some of the structural challenges the U.S. economy faces, from labor shortages to stagnant productivity growth, positioning the market for another wave of strong returns.

The U.S. Economy's Resilience: Overcoming Adversity

Throughout U.S. history, the stock market has shown remarkable spirit in the face of adversity. Whether it was the Great Depression, World War II, or the 2008 financial crisis, the market has not only recovered from these periods of turmoil but has often emerged stronger. The generational cycles discussed in this book underscore the fact that market downturns, while painful, are part of the natural rhythm of financial markets.

The COVID-19 pandemic provided the most recent example of this strength. In early 2020, as the global economy ground to a halt and millions of people lost their lives or livelihoods, the stock market plunged. However, within months, thanks to unprecedented fiscal and monetary stimulus, technological adaptation, and the resilience of the American economy, the market rebounded to new highs. The rapid development and distribution of vaccines in 2021 underscored the importance of innovation and global cooperation in overcoming challenges. The stock market's swift recovery from the pandemic illustrates once again that, even in the face of global crises, the market continues to move forward, driven by human ingenuity and determination.

This capacity to rebound from crises is not new. The 2008 financial crisis, for example, wiped out trillions of dollars in wealth and left millions unemployed, but it also led to the rise of new technologies, stronger financial regulations, and a decade-long bull market that rewarded those who remained invested. Every contraction has its lessons, and every expansion brings new opportunities.

The Generational Cycles: A Guide for Investors

By studying the generational cycles of the stock market, investors can better understand the forces that drive market movements and prepare themselves for future challenges. In the contractionary periods, risk management, diversification, and patience are essential. In expansionary periods, it is innovation, adaptability, and forward-looking investment strategies that provide the greatest rewards. Each cycle brings its own opportunities and risks, but the long-term history of the market remains clear: upward and to the right.

As we look to the future, with AI, automation, and other technological advancements on the horizon, there is every reason to believe that the next expansion cycle will bring with it opportunities for growth and wealth creation. Just as the industrial revolution and the rise of the internet transformed the global economy in previous cycles, AI has the potential to reshape industries, improve productivity, and unlock new sources of value. Investors who understand the short term cycles of the markets, keep in mind the Generational Cycles, and embrace the opportunities presented by these technological advancements will be well-positioned to benefit from the next wave of growth.

Conclusion: Hopeful for the Future

As we conclude this exploration of the U.S. stock market's Generational Cycles and history, we can take solace in the fact that, despite the challenges we have faced as a nation—from financial crises to pandemics—the market has always found a way to recover and thrive. The cycles of expansion and contraction are not only natural but essential to the process of growth and innovation. Each contraction has paved the way for a stronger expansion, and each expansion has brought new technologies, opportunities, and improvements in our quality of life.

The rise of AI and other emerging technologies offers the promise of a new era of productivity, efficiency, and wealth creation. While there will undoubtedly be challenges along the way, the lessons from previous years remind us that perseverance, adaptability, and innovation are the keys to long-term success. Over the past 114 years, the U.S. economy and stock market have shown time and time again the ability to bounce back, and there is every reason to believe that they will continue to do so in the decades to come.

In conclusion, the U.S. stock market's history is not just a story of numbers and financial charts; it's a reflection of broader societal and economic forces. Markets move in rhythms, shaped by the events, innovations, and decisions of each era. The generational cycles that have defined the market over the past century will continue to shape its future, and by learning from the past, we can be better prepared for whatever waves the market brings next.

Made in the USA
Columbia, SC
21 October 2024